ALCOTT'S NEW SERIES.

FAMILIAR LETTERS

TO

YOUNG MEN

ON

VARIOUS SUBJECTS.

DESIGNED AS A

Companion to the Young Man's Guide.

BY

WM. A. ALCOTT,
AUTHOR OF THE 'YOUNG MOTHER,' 'YOUNG HUSBAND,'
ETC., ETC.

BUFFALO:
GEO. H. DERBY AND CO.
1850.

JOHN F. TROW,
Printer and Stereotyper,
49 and 51 Ann-st., N. Y.

TO THE READER.

In the Preface to the "Young Man's Guide," first edition, the reader may find the following paragraph, which will be a sufficient apology—if apology is needed—for the appearance of the present volume.

"Nor is it to be expected that a work of this size would make the lofty pretensions of embracing every thing which it is necessary for young men to know and practise in order to become useful, virtuous and happy, in all the relations of life. A few topics only have been presented; and those with a brevity which, I fear, will detract from their importance. Should the work, however, meet the approbation of those for whom it is intended, and be a means of improving their character, it is not improbable that *another volume*, embracing several other important and interesting topics which were necessarily excluded from this, may hereafter be attempted."

Now if the sale of about 50,000 of the "Young Man's Guide," during the past fifteen years, requires that I should redeem the pledge thus publicly and voluntarily given, I herewith make the attempt. But I do so in part only; for there remains a wide range of subjects belonging to the department of Health and Physiology, as necessary to young men as any thing I have yet written; which may possibly bring me, once more, before the many millions of a class of citizens for whom well written books, in the right style and spirit, are, at the present crisis, most imperiously demanded.

I should also observe, in this place, that some of the following letters, in a crude form, have already appeared in the columns of the New-York Evangelist and other papers and journals. In the present case, however, they are considerably altered, amended, and, as I trust, improved.

THE AUTHOR.

West Newton, Mass., June, **1849.**

CONTENTS.

LETTER I.

PRELIMINARY REMARKS.

LETTER II.

SELF-RESPECT AND SELF-REVERENCE.

LETTER III.

SELF-KNOWLEDGE.

LETTER IV.

SELF-DEPENDENCE.

CONTENTS.

LETTER XI.

THE LOVE AND SPIRIT OF PROGRESS.

LETTER XII.

LOVE OF INQUIRY; OR, FREE-THINKING.

LETTER XIII.

RIGHT USE OF OURSELVES.

LETTER XIV.

PHYSIOLOGY.

LETTER XV.

PHRENOLOGY.

CONTENTS.

LETTER XVI.

PHYSIOGNOMY.

LETTER XVII.

TRAVELLING.

LETTER XVIII.

CONSCIENTIOUSNESS.

LETTER XIX.

LOVE OF EXCITEMENT.

LETTER XX.

ON PURITY.

LETTER XXVII.

RESPECT FOR AGE.

LETTER XXVIII.

DUTIES TO THE AGED.

LETTER XXIX.

POLITICS AND POLITICAL DUTIES.

LETTER XXX.

FEMALE SOCIETY.

LETTER XXXI.

GENERAL DUTY OF MARRIAGE.

LETTER XXXII.

RELIGION AND SKEPTICISM.

LETTER XXXIII.

THE CHRISTIAN RELIGION.

LETTER XXXIV.

DEATH AND FUTURITY.

LETTERS TO YOUNG MEN.

LETTER I.

PRELIMINARY REMARKS.

In addressing young men as a class, it is difficult to fix the mind's eye on any particular age. There is a period—and it arrives sooner in the lives of some, and later in those of others—when they may be said to begin to act for themselves; and in the common but not inappropriate language of the day, to form their own character. They are indeed forming character by every action of every day of their lives, whether that action be of the voluntary or of the involuntary kind. When, however, in these communications, I shall speak to you of forming your own characters, or of educating yourselves, reference will be had principally to those acts which seem to be almost if not quite without the pale of the family, and beyond parental control;—those acts in whicn and by which every young man practically says, "I take the responsibility."

The prevalent custom of singling out young men and addressing them, has not originated in the belief that they arrive earlier or with less experience at the period of life of which I have been speaking than formerly—though this probably is the fact—but rather from the conviction that their responsibilities, when assumed, are more weighty. They are also believed to be more exposed to temptation than formerly, both physically and morally. Besides, the world is learning at last—though even now very slowly—the vast superiority of prevention, whenever and wherever it can be applied, to correction or cure.

Young men are ever inexperienced—it must be so in the nature of things—and therefore ever apt to be thoughtless. And with them, when they *do* think, the golden age stands out in the future—not as with old men, in the past. It is well indeed it should be so. The world is certainly onward—progressive—even though it should make but *slow* progress. He, then, who places the golden age in the future, is correct. Besides this, young men require the stimulus of high hope in order to the best development and most favorable exercise of their powers and capacities.

My counsel to the young, then, always is: Expect great things in the future. Expect, even, *to do great things yourselves.* It is necessary to aim high, were it only to accomplish a little. But no young man has a moral right to satisfy, if he could, the desires of his immortal mind, and the requirements of society and of God, by merely expecting to accomplish a little. He is bound to expect much, and attempt much.

Some young men have done this, to their honor, in every age. It is those alone who have thus expected and acted, who have shone as lights in the world. And they have had their reward. And what young men *have* done in the past, young men *can* do in the present and future.

But if these counsels are adapted to young men generally, they are peculiarly so to those of United America. It is not too much to say, that at every period of our history as a republic, the young have held in their own hands, at least prospectively, our national destinies. They have—practically so, at least—elected several of our chief magistrates already.

Besides, in no country of the known world—the world past or present—have the "counsels" of old men so early required the "activities" of the young, as in the United States. In this respect it is that, under the genius of civil institutions like our own, the young may be said to be the rulers of the land.

This is republicanism with twofold force. One might think it enough that power should have passed from the few to the many; from the king and nobility to the subjects and people; but when the crown is not only transferred to the people, but to the *young* people, it introduces quite a new order of things.

Happy, then, the people whose youthful rulers—for such the young men of our land are daily and hourly becoming—are duly qualified to rule in wisdom and in the fear of the Lord. But woe to that country and that people whose young men hearken not to the counsels of the old, nor rise up at their presence. Theirs may indeed be republicanism—the semblance of it—but then it is republicanism in its worst form. It is republicanism "with a vengeance."

The time *has been* when our young men were treated with too much reserve, and kept at too great a distance; when, in truth, not a few were treated more like servants and menials than like sons. But "times are altered." And in passing, as we now are, to the other extreme, it may be worth while to inquire whether there is not danger of going too far.

For what means the claim which has not only been made in every past age but in our own, with a voice, as it were, of authority, that the old were fools, and that only "present times are wise?" What means the tendency which is every where obvious, not only to use the young for action, but for counsel too? Or has there been, of late, some new dispensation which changes the relation of young men, and without the pain of acquiring experience, imparts its privileges?

It is said, I know, that old men not only forget that they themselves have once been young, but claim superior wisdom at the precise time when they manifest the want of it. But is not this to beg the very question in debate? Is it not to assume what the young, of course, cannot prove?

Grant that age is not always wise, or even experienced, is not youth, of necessity, destitute of that experience which, if it does not always impart wisdom, always may do it? And if a few old men who set up their claims for wisdom and experience are mere "croakers," are they all so? Do not some of them still sympathize with childhood and youth? And may not—should not—childhood and youth avail themselves of this sympathy?

I have said that the responsibilities of young men are more weighty than formerly. Does such a position need any farther elucidation? If young men are, prospectively, and indeed in reality, the rulers of our land, are not their responsibilities weighty? Nor are they diminished by the rising conviction on the public mind of these youthful rulers, that old men, of the present age, at least, are but old fools.

Besides, it cannot be overlooked by any young man who takes the pains to reflect a moment, or even to read what I am writing, that if young men do hold in their hands the destinies of our country, they also hold in their hands, at the same time, the destinies of all our institutions, social, literary, and religious.

I have said that you are more exposed to temptation, my young friends, than formerly. There are various reasons why this should be so. In the first place, your internal organization is less favorable for the mighty work of resisting temptation, than the organization of young men in past times. This, I must ask you to take, now, for granted; reserving for the present the task of proving what I have asserted. Then, in the second place, civilization and refinement are on the march; but these, while they place us within the range both of better and worse influences, according to our taste and option, do not necessarily give us greater power to resist temptation or oppose downward tendencies; whether these last arise from external circumstances, or from the internal current of that common depravity of which we all partake.

Thirdly, you are more exposed to temptation than young men formerly were, because you have more leisure than they had. I need not repeat to you the old adage concerning the prince of availables, and his readiness to make the idle man his workshop. In former times, moreover, there were fewer holidays than now, and those holidays were spent in a very different manner.

Lastly, it should be remembered that labor-saving machinery—including, of course, the canal, the railroad, the steamboat, and the telegraph—while it brings us countless blessings in its train, imparts also the power as well as the temptation to wrong-doing, and to the misrule both of your own spirits, and of that society over whom Providence has placed you.

I asked a distinguished phrenologist, one

day, why he was so apt to dwell on the good traits in the character of those whose heads he examined. His reply was, "Because it is needful to inspire young men with confidence in themselves. They do not think how much they might accomplish, if they would but try. They are wanting—the truly capable ones at least—in self-respect and self-reverence."

There was truth in his remark; and this is one reason why I have said so much, both here and elsewhere, to young men. But on the subject of self-reverence and self-respect, I must speak in my next letter.

LETTER II.

SELF-RESPECT AND SELF-REVERENCE.

"I do and must reverence human nature," said an eminent New England divine; but in saying this the doctor exposed himself greatly to criticism. Indeed, I was inclined to wonder at the expression myself. So long and so justly had I regarded human nature as perverted and fallen, that I almost forgot that there were, so to speak, two sides to it; that if on the one side we are allied to the worm, and even to the dust we tread on, it is not less true that we are, on the other side, allied to angels, and cherubs, and seraphs, and even to the great God himself. And yet that such is the fact, who will presume to deny?

We reverence our parents, and sometimes

our rulers, especially when we regard them as ruling us in righteousness; and is there aught in this to which the most fastidious or sensitive could well object? Then why should we shrink from the idea of reverencing human nature?

For in so doing, it is not necessary that we should reverence human nature in all its depraved forms. We only reverence it as it should be, and for the sake of those important relations and responsibilities which it was originally intended to sustain. We reverence it, in part, for the sake of the Divine image which was originally enstamped on it.

For you will not doubt that we are the children of one common Father, or that though we have strayed from this Father's house we are still his children, and treated by him as such. And is not provision made—has it not been made these 1800 years—for restoring in us that resemblance to our heavenly Father which we have lost by our transgressions?

Addison, in the Spectator, has somewhere intimated that the time may come in eternity, when the meanest redeemed human soul will rise as much higher in the scale of moral excellence and glory, than the post now occupied by Gabriel, as that bright seraph is exalted above the lowest of the Hottentots, or even of the savages of the wilderness. And an authority higher than Addison has said: "Eye hath not seen, ear hath not heard, neither hath it entered into the heart of man to conceive the things which God hath prepared for them that love him."

Think, too, of a Newton, a Franklin, or a Herschel. We are accustomed to regard these men as giants in point of intellect. And, compared with the mass of mankind around them, they were so. Who does not reverence them —their nature at the least? Yet what were these men in comparison with what they might have been, could life have been prolonged to them a thousand years, to what in truth they may yet become? Did they not think meanly of themselves, when they thought of the amazing heights of science which neither they nor any other mortals had yet climbed?

Yet what were Newton, La Place, Franklin, Cuvier, Solomon, even, considered merely as men of learning or as intellectual giants, when compared with John, and Paul, and Brainard, and Howard? What is mere intellectual greatness to moral elevation? And why might we not have the union of both these in the same individual? Suppose for once the union were to take place. Suppose a Paul, with his moral greatness, superadded to a Sir Isaac Newton. The thing is quite conceivable. Who would not reverence such a character? And is not human nature, thus elevated, ennobled, and rendered godlike, worthy to be reverenced?

But to these sublime heights, O young man—these portals of celestial day, as the poet calls them—it is your privilege no less than your duty to aspire. You cannot know that you may not, at some day, by the full development and cultivation of all your powers, faculties and functions, rise to those heights, whence you may look down on all who have lived before you, and even on Gabriel and all the cherubim and seraphim that stand before the throne eternal.

Will you not, then, learn to reverence yourselves, or at least that wonderful nature with which God in his Providence has intrusted you? Will you dare to degrade, in any conceivable way, a nature allied to angels and archangels, and to the Eternal himself? Made to belong to the divine family—to be among the sons and daughters of the Lord Almighty—will you presume to sink yourself to the level, and below the level, of the brutes that perish?

Learn then to respect—to reverence—thyself. Learn to reverence thyself for the sake of thyself. Made to be like the sons of God, and to dwell in their midst—nay, to be as it were a son of God thyself—wilt thou lose a single opportunity for qualifying thyself, intellectually, morally, or even physically, for that blest abode? Wilt thou not exert every faculty and every power, to the full extent of those faculties and powers, to become what thou wilt wish hereafter thou hadst made thyself?

Thyself, *physically*. This may seem to thee a riddle. But I will endeavor to make it more plain hereafter. In the meantime read the fifteenth chapter of Paul's first letter to his Corinthian brethren. There will be found a partial solution of what may, at first view, seem enigmatical in this particular.

Learn, above all, to reverence thyself for the sake of Him who is at once thy Creator, thy Preserver, thy Redeemer; and what is more —I was going to say infinitely more—interesting, thy Father. Oh! what a word is this, thy everlasting Father! Should a son of the eternal God ever cease to reverence himself? Should he ever for one short moment forget his royal birth and blood? Should he not live and die with the highest hopes, the highest aspirations, the highest self-reverence?

LETTER III.

SELF-KNOWLEDGE.

In order to *reverence* himself, a young man must first *know* himself. I do not mean by this, that he must know himself as thoroughly as God knows him; for that were an impossibility. Nor do I mean to intimate that his knowledge of himself must be fully acquired at once. All I mean to affirm is, that the reverence of ourselves, which was urged in the last Letter, will always be graduated by our self-knowledge.

True it is that a due reverence of ourselves would be a most commanding motive to every young man in the pursuit of self-knowledge. The maxim, or injunction, "Know thyself," coming down to us, as it does, from the remotest antiquity, and urged and echoed from the pages of all wisdom sacred and profane, strikes us with greater or less force in proportion as we are more or less acquainted already, with the subject to which our attention is directed.

"To know ourselves diseased is half our cure," is often and well said. It is also said that they only who are sick, feel the need of a physician. Now we are all sick in this particular, if in no other, that we are all vastly ignorant of ourselves. We are not very profound in the knowledge of others; but as regards the knowledge of ourselves, we are greatly deficient. Here the wisest of us might well take lessons.

And herein consists the greatest hinderance to self-knowledge, viz.; that we do not know, as Dr. Watts aptly expresses it, how weak and unwise we are. We may acknowledge ourselves ignorant, at least before God; but we seldom really *feel* our ignorance. Somehow or other we still cling to the idea that we are pretty wise, after all.

Talk to a young man of his ignorance. If you are an elder, he admits it. But suppose you are his equal, real or supposed—what then? Possibly he may *seem* to admit it; but in the far greater majority of cases he will repel the idea; in too many instances with emotions of anger, if not with violence. I have seen many a young man who would bear with composure, almost any charge, except that of ignorance of himself, or of his own nature. And more, still—as if to atone for their ignorance, will say, bloatingly, "Human nature, I think, is the greatest study, after all."

The truth is, that the more ignorant we are, in this particular, the greater our confidence in the extent of our self-knowledge. And on the contrary, the more truly wise we are, the more clearly we perceive the depths of our ignorance, on all subjects, but especially in regard to ourselves. One of the greatest obstacles to human progress, as I have already more than intimated, consists in this, that we are not yet wise and learned enough, either individually or collectively, to perceive the necessity of self-exertion, or to value its rewards. We are not wise enough, in other words, to know how ignorant we are.

Concerning this subject—self-knowledge—in regard to its importance to young men, I feel incompetent to speak, on account of its magnitude. The language of Holy Writ, in relation to another matter, seems to repel me:—It is high as heaven, what canst thou do? it is deep as hell, what canst thou know?

The young man, no less than the old one, has a threefold nature—is a trinity in unity—like his Maker. A knowledge of this great fact is of the first importance in the outset, because it involves high and important duties. If our nature is made up, as Paul would intimate, of body, soul, and spirit, or, as the moderns express it, of physical, intellectual and moral powers, then in order to know ourselves correctly, we must know something of each of these great departments of our nature, as well as of their relations to each other and to the beings and things around us.

But this knowledge, so essential to the young man, in all past ages—and little less in the present—is denied him. Not, indeed, by design, with malice aforethought, open or covert, but by the construction and arrangement of society. It is so in the nature of things.

The first part of his nature which is recognized as worthy of cultivation, is his memory. At home or abroad, he is thought to be learned, in proportion to the load of words—the signs of other men's ideas—which he can be made to carry. And when he seems to rise to the cultivation of other and higher faculties, it is ten to one, but his instruction consists of mere memory work. The other faculties of our intellectual domain are undeveloped, and consequently uncultivated.

But if the various mental faculties lie hidden from young men, at least for the far greater part, how much more so the relations of these faculties to each other! Intellectual Philosophy is a term with whose *meaning*, even, young men are scarcely made acquainted. The dependence of a good judgment upon accurate perception, patient attention, careful comparison, and the proper and natural association of our ideas, is a thing of which the young man, unless by sheer accident, is almost as ignorant as the merest savage, or as the "man in the moon."

Still more rarely is it made a fundamental point, in early education, to watch the operations of the mind, and learn to analyze one's ideas. Indeed this busy age seems altogether unfavorable to much reflection, so that if it were taught us in the schools, it would not be likely to thrive out of them. Steamboats, railroads, and electro-magnetic telegraphs are not in this respect very favorable.

It is sometimes said that a person ought not to know, by his sensations or feelings, that he *has* a stomach. Now if it were the great purpose of all those who have the care of the young, to cultivate their minds—rather to *pretend* to cultivate them—in such a way that they may never know they *have* any *minds*, it would be difficult to devise a better system for this purpose than that which so extensively prevails among us.

And then the moral part of the young man—does this receive any better attention than the intellectual? Do the young know that they have a moral nature? If so, how come they by the knowledge? Is it obtainable in the family? Is it found in the schools? By what processes are the young, of each successive rising generation, made to know something of the healthful nature and tendencies of the elevating affections and passions, as love, hope, joy, peace, cheerfulness, &c., or of the unfavorable tendency of their opposites, such as hatred, despondency, grief, anger, melancholy, &c.?

The instructions of the family, the common school, the high school, and the Sabbath school, do much for us, I admit; but what do they in the way of teaching us ourselves? Even the Sabbath school, whose special prerogative it would appear to be to unveil to us ourselves and our relations to our neighbor and to God, informs us of every thing else rather than this most important of all knowledge. In this, even, what is told us is often made to play "round the head," but comes not to the heart."

This omission, I admit, is not from a settled intention to avoid the knowledge of ourselves. By no means. On the other hand. however, it is not from a settled intention to *communicate* that knowledge. And this it is that I complain of as unworthy of the times we live in, and the glorious light which has risen upon us. The knowledge of ourselves is the foundation—or should be—of all other knowledge, earthly or heavenly. And it is for want of this knowledge, at least in part, that mankind are such bundles, so to speak, of inconsistencies as render human character strangely enigmatical, when it should be the reverse.

Granted, however, that the young were trained to a knowledge of themselves, intellectually and morally, as they ought to be. Granted that every thing received the measure of attention it deserves in the two great departments of the human domain to which I have adverted. Still, what is known of the physical part of us—the body, so fearfully and wonderfully made? What know we of its nature, functions, relations, and purposes?

We explore the vast domain of external nature, unhesitatingly. We become acquainted with the geography, the geology, the history of the world in which we live. We study natural history—animals, vegetables, and minerals. To find the latter, we dig deep in the bowels of the earth, or perseveringly drain, as it were, one by one, her sands. We ascend the heavens, as aeronauts; or, by aid of telescopes of mighty power, explore sun, moon, and stars. Or, aided by lightning speed, we canvass the actions of men hundreds or thousands of miles distant, if perchance we may understand them, and read their hearts by their lives. And yet, after having explored and analyzed our own and other worlds, we come back utterly ignorant, for the most part, of the very house we live in—the house of the soul—the fearfully and wonderfully organized body. Nor do we know much, if indeed any thing, more of its relations to the mind—the spiritual inhabitant—that occupies it.

Or, to use the still more expressive language of another writer, "Why is not the science of physiology taught in all our colleges? Astronomy, natural philosophy, chemistry, mineralogy, geology, and botany, are not neglected. Students are required to become familiar with the air they breathe, the water they drink, the fire that warms them, and the dust they tread on. They must know something, forsooth, about "spots on the sun," eclipses, "northern lights," meteoric stones, the "milky way," the great bear, the little bear, comets' tails, Saturn's rings, and Jupiter's moons. They must know all about the variations of the needle, the tides, the trade winds, the Gulf Stream, the phenomena of earthquakes, thunder, volcanic eruptions, why a stone falls *down* rather than *up*, and what flattened the poles.

"All this is very well. But what do our graduates generally know of the structure *of their bodies*, the functions of the different organs, and their laws of relation? Just about as much as the Peripatetics did of ideas, when they supposed them little filmy things that floated off from objects, and somehow wormed their way through the senses, and finally stuck fast on the pineal gland of the brain, like barnacles.

"Modern education conducts the student round the universe; bids him scale the heights of nature, and drop his fathom line among the deep soundings of her abyss, compassing the vast, and analyzing the minute, and yet never conducts him over the boundary of that world of living wonders which constitutes him *man*, and is at once the abode of his mind, the instrument of its action, and the subject of its sway. Why, I ask, shall every thing else be studied, while the human frame is passed over as a noteless, forgotten thing?—that masterpiece of divine mechanism, pronounced by its Author "wonderfully made" and "curiously wrought," a temple fitted up by God, and gloriously garnished for the residence of an immortal inhabitant, bearing his own image, and a candi date for "a building of God, eternal in the heavens."

Thousands of students are now prosecuting a course of study in our higher seminaries, which occupies from six to nine years. Why are not a few months set apart for studying the architecture of this "earthly house of our tabernacle," its simplicity, its beauty, its harmony, its grandeur, its majestic perfection?

Is there not something which is peculiarly unaccountable—passing strange—in the state of things here alluded to? And is it not still more strange, if possible, that it should be suffered to remain; that mankind, professing to be guided by reason, are so very unreasonable as to study and explore and form an intimate acquaintance with every thing around them, rather than with themselves? That they should be willing to spend thirty, fifty, or seventy years in this way, and even go down to the grave almost without the slightest knowledge of the framework of their own bodies? Grant that matters are in this respect improving, they are by no means as they should be.

Young man, by these remarks, I beseech thee to be admonished. Invert not, thus, the whole order of things, as the Creator established, or at least designed them. Know thyself. Know every thing if thou canst—every thing, I mean, which is worth knowing. But remember one thing, in passing. Remember that though science and art are long, life at best is short; that whatever is worth doing should be done with all thy might. That it must, moreover, if done at all, be done quickly; since there is neither knowledge nor device in the grave, whither thou art fast hastening. Remember thou art fearfully made up of body, mind and spirit; that thy first duty is to become acquainted, as much as thou mayest, with these—their structure, offices, laws, and relations; and with the relation of them, when combined, to thy fellow beings, and thy Eternal Father. Remember, therefore, I again say, whatever else thou knowest, less or more, know thou thyself.

Shall I proffer thee aids in this work? God hath provided them to thy hand already. David, the shepherd king of Israel, appears to have studied the heavens as well as the earth, while watching his father's numerous flocks on the plains of Judea. Furnished with light which David never had, thou knowest enough of thyself, already, to begin the great work. Half the wonders of thy frame--the house thou occupiest—lie open to the most careless observer, who observes at all; and what is not obvious to thine own ingenuity, the labors of others will readily supply. Works on Anatomy, Physiology, and Hygiene, in various shapes, suited to thy capacity, are within thy reach. Then there are Watts on the Mind,

Mason on Self-Knowledge, the works of Dick, the Combes, and a host of others; and last, but not least, the Bible.

Here, after all, is the great volume on Self-Knowledge—so plain, that he who runs may read—so ample, that it touches every case, of every individual, of all ages and climes—so satisfactory, that he who acts in its spirit will never fail to know himself, to reverence himself, and to transmit himself to coming ages.

Young men place the golden age in the future, and well they may. The study of ourselves, in the fullest, largest sense, will enable us to enjoy, at least in prospect, all that poets have dreamed of in the future, and all that philosophy, even Bible Philosophy, has painted on the portals of heaven. Know then thyself.

Ignorant of thyself, thou knowest nothing as thou oughtest to know. Know thyself, and thou knowest all else which is necessary. Know thyself, and obey thyself; know thy relations and duties to all within, around, and above thee, and nothing can harm thee either in this world or in the world which is to come.

LETTER IV.

SELF-DEPENDENCE.

THERE is a wide difference, my young friends, between Self-Dependence and Self-Confidence. A good measure, it is true, even of this last, should be in the possession of every young person, in order to success in life. I have spoken of this before; but you will allow me to advert to it once more.

I have known a young man, eighteen or twenty years of age, who was as destitute of confidence in himself as the veriest child. Though he was by no means wanting in the power to accomplish what he undertook, yet such had been his training, that he shrunk from every thing which was new to him, or which presented but the slightest difficulties.

This unhappy state of things, as I have already said, was the result of wrong training. The father was in the habit of taking it for granted that his son was somewhat wanting in the capacity to accomplish any thing, and the son knew it. And, as usually happens in such cases, what he *took* the son to be, he insensibly *became*. Or if he did not deteriorate, there was a tendency to deterioration.

Another young man, in the same neighborhood, had been treated in a manner entirely different. He had, in early life, lost both his parents, and having a character, by constitution, somewhat versatile, the circumstances and changes to which he had been subjected had made him a perfect Alcibiades. He could *be* or *do*, as he thought, almost any thing he pleased. And this confidence in himself was so great, as in some instances to secure the point, and enable him to execute what never could have been accomplished otherwise.

One day, in the time of sheep-shearing, he was passing a yard where an experienced individual was engaged in shearing sheep. A person who stood looking on, and who knew the drift of the young man, called out, "Henry, can you shear sheep?" "Oh yes," was the reply. "Did you ever shear any?" "Often," said he. "Come, then," said the man with the shears, "and make the attempt."

Henry did not hesitate. He was, however, only about sixteen years of age; had just come from the city; and, it was quite probable, had never seen a sheep sheared, before, in his life. For it is almost unnecessary to say that situated as he had been, he had learned one thing—the art of telling a falsehood very smoothly.

To the surprise, however, of all, he succeeded very well. And his success was owing, in part at least, to his self-confidence. The young man of twenty, of whom I have already spoken, stood by, and was as much surprised as any of the company; for though brought up in a land of flocks and herds, he would have no more thought of shearing a sheep, than of going, even at that time, to California.

Self-confidence in excess, however, is as injurious as its opposite—extreme distrust or diffidence. Self-dependence, on the other hand, can hardly be in excess, in any possible instance. The more of it, the better. Thousands, at least, suffer for want of a due proportion of this rare quality, to one for too much of it. McClure, the geologist, insists that it is on this account, in part, that orphans make their way best in the world. But orphans *do not make their way best.*

Some, indeed, viewing the matter religiously, might imagine evil as the result of large self-dependence. But I am not speaking here of the dependence we should have on ourselves, as opposed to the dependence we should have on our parents, or on others; much less on God. I suppose, however, that the more truly self-dependent we are, in a religious sense, the more truly shall we depend on a heavenly Father; and, on the contrary, the less we depend on ourselves, the less shall we depend on God. For he only has these opposites in just measure, who is in harmony with himself and with all other things; and the truly religious man is, after all, the only man of true harmony.

If we could contrive some way to throw the young upon their own resources, or, in other words, render them self-dependent, and at the same time make them feel their own littleness and dependence, a most important point would be gained to the cause of education, and the happiness of each rising generation greatly augmented. But to unite these two, if indeed they can be united, seems to be reserved for remote generations.

I love to see a young man modest, and even diffident; and yet I love to see him self-confident to a considerable extent, and self-dependent, very largely. Without self-confidence and self-dependence, he will hardly make much progress in the world—with them, he will hardly fail to go forward, in some direction or another.

He will be, in fact, much like a ship at sea, with a fair wind. If she has a good pilot, she will probably reach the desired haven; if otherwise, there can be no certainty on this subject. So with a young man. If his head be a wise helmsman, he will come out safe; but if not, he may suffer a most dangerous, if not fatal shipwreck.

In any event—I repeat the remark—I love to

find a young man really and truly self-dependent. I love to have him feel as if he could be and do any thing that was ever done by man. I do not mean by this, that he should feel as if he could do all things equally well, or even as well as some others; but I do desire to see every young man "going ahead."

The rich young man is not likely to be self-dependent. Things have been done *for* him too much. He has never felt want. Of course he has never enjoyed the pleasure of providing, by his own efforts of body or mind, for his own necessities. Whether a student, a laborer, a merchant, a mechanic or a manufacturer, he will hardly succeed in accomplishing much, because he has never been taught the very first lesson.

This is one of the great evils of riches—not that it spoils the possessor himself, though this were bad enough, but that it spoils his children. Or if there be exceptions to the truth of this remark, they are few and far between.

The indigent man is not much better off, however. His poverty is apt to create in him meanness of spirit. Hence the wisdom of

Agur's prayer of old—"Give me neither poverty nor riches." If Agur, at his time of life, was likely to be tempted to mean or dishonest acts by poverty, it is not likely the young can escape. But this meanness to which I allude—the exact opposite of what was alluded to in a former paragraph—is entirely unfavorable to true self-dependence.

I do not mean to say, or to intimate, that the quality to which I refer is *never* found in either a rich or poor young man; but only that both riches and poverty present or bring with them their difficulties. That they are occasionally surmounted by genius, and even by other circumstances, is most cheerfully admitted.

The remarks which have been made in regard to the two extremes of poverty and riches, in their effects on the self-dependence of young men, may be applied to many other circumstances and conditions of human life. Perhaps we may profitably spend a few moments on this topic.

Rank is unfavorable to self-dependence. Thus he who, by birth, is made lord, or duke, or even esquire, is thereby absolved—I mean practically—from the duty of self exertion. He is not likely to rise to the condition of monarch on the one hand, do what he may, nor is he much more likely to sink to the condition of serf or peasant on the other.

And then the latter—the individual who in a country of lords and tenants, is born at the lower extreme of society—what can *he* do? For it is not possible, in one case in a million, that he should rise above his rank. And stupid as he is, he generally knows it, and governs himself accordingly.

I have seen the slave in the service of his master. What motive had he to self-dependence? He must depend on his master. For let him make ever so much exertion, become ever so active or enterprising, and he is still but a slave, and as a general rule must expect to remain so.

What a blessed thing it is to be born in a country, where riches and poverty, and rank and caste have not produced their worst effects —and where slavery even is not as yet universal! What a favor to be born in the United States of America! That things are not as they should be, even here, is most readily and fully conceded. That the spirit of wealth, rank and caste are abroad, and on the increase among us, is most certain. That the circumstances into which the young man is introduced at birth, are, in many respects, greatly unfavorable to self-dependence, cannot be denied. Still it would be difficult for the young to improve their condition in this particular, by going to another country. For whither shall they go? Here, the road is open to riches, honors, preferment. Every young man may be an Astor, a Polk, a Franklin or a Dwight—just as he pleases; provided he will make such exertion as God and nature and circumstances have placed within his reach and power.

Need I repeat the exhortation to the young to avail themselves of the circumstances and privileges thus allotted them? Need I urge them to remember that they are born, not in the twelfth or the sixteenth century, nor in

South Africa or in New Zealand, nor even in Oregon or California, but in the nineteenth century, and in the United States of America?

LETTER V.

SELF-EDUCATION.

In a preceding letter, I have more than intimated that the great business of young men is the formation of right character for noble ends; in other words, self-education. For what is this world; what is human life, at least in its earliest stages, but a great school of education? Nay, I might even ask, were this the appropriate place for it, What is Christianity itself but a system—a set of lessons, so to speak—prepared by Heaven for the purpose of making men—and the young, of course—wiser and better?

My purpose, at the present time, will be to say something about the means and processes of this self-education—this formation of character—more especially beyond the precincts of the family circle, and the domain of family influences. And in the first place, allow me to speak of what I choose to call *harmony*.

By harmony in the formation of character, I mean such a development of the individual as will produce uniformity. Every young man understands the term in its application to a musical performance, as well as to architecture. Yet as surely as a piece of music should be harmonious, or the various parts of an edifice or temple in due proportion and harmony, so should the human character—the Christian temple. In truth, a want of harmony in the latter case is as much more to be deplored, as the imperishable is more valuable than the perishable.

Man's nature, as I have before said, is not simple and uncompounded. It is in the image of its Divine author. Man is made up of body, soul, and spirit, as Paul has it; or of body, head, and heart, as the moderns. In either case the idea is the same; man is at once a physical, intellectual, and moral being.

Now, in order to produce a harmonious development of human character, as well as harmonious results, all these departments, so to call them, of human nature, must be properly developed and cultivated. If this is done, and done early, the result is what might be called —what is called in fact—a proper balance. Thus a harmonious character is a well-balanced character.

But where shall we go, it may be asked, to find such a character—an individual, young or old, in whom body, head and heart, are proportionally developed and cultivated? Men in all ages and climes, and under every dispensation, have been but mere fragments of men. To point to one harmonious character —perfectly so—would be to point to something beyond the precincts of either sacred or profane history.

Acknowledged. "No mere man"—none but the God-man—has been found to come up to this beau-ideal of perfect humanity. But what then? Because man has never come up to the dignity of his nature, does it follow that he never will do it?

That we know not yet what we shall or

can be, is alike the language of religion and philosophy. Suppose, however, it were not so; suppose, as I believe to be true, that men have hitherto been mere fragments of men, is it not equally true—is it not even certain—that the larger fragments, or rather those which embraced the greatest number of elements belonging to the common mass, have been most useful?

If it should be argued that young men, such as I am addressing, are not expected to have those well-balanced natures which farther education and a more extended experience would be apt to develope—that indeed they cannot have them—I should meet the argument by a flat and positive denial. Your character should be as harmonious at four as at sixteen, and at sixteen as at sixty. It should be in harmony at every age of moral accountability, and in all circumstances. And if the rabbins and teachers of this or any other age or clime have taught otherwise, this does not alter the matter of fact. "To the law and to the testimony."

One reason why men have been hitherto

so little harmonious in their character, may be, that society, as a whole, has been inharmonious. Society—civilized society I here mean more particularly—like the individuals of which it is made up, is unequally and inharmoniously developed in the very best circumstances.

Sometimes the intellectual part is greatly in advance of the moral; perhaps even of the physical. In other instances it may be the moral predominates, or at least leads. More commonly, however, the physical part of the social system is greatly in advance of all the rest. Such is the fact—most strikingly so—at the present moment. Nor is this the worst. The wonderful progress of labor-saving machinery and the arts is greatly increasing this preponderance.

Now the greater this want of harmony in human society, considered as one huge individual, the greater the tendency to a want of harmony in the individuals of which it is composed. Some have even said that this tendency is inevitable. I do not so regard it, however. Man is not a mere machine. To his machinery is superadded free agency; and this enables him not only to control matter, and hold in abeyance some of the laws and tendencies of matter, but even to turn them to a good account.

This view of the case, young men, indicates your true position in civil society. You inherit an inharmonious tendency to begin with. Then, as you pass on through infancy and childhood to youth and adolescence, your education but serves to confirm what has been so inauspiciously begun. Your appetites are misdirected, your physical powers in general perverted or misemployed, and your pampered bodies either stinted on the one hand, in a greater or less degree, or on the other hand pushed to giant size or diseased fulness.

Meanwhile, by neglect, your mind and heart suffer; or, if otherwise, their growth is sickly. For the law of organized bodies, as yet but faintly alluded to, that if one member suffers all the members suffer with it, is as applicable to the three departments of man's nature of which I have already spoken, as to those subdivisions of each to which I shall hereafter call your attention.

Is any individual discouraged by the views I have suggested? I trust otherwise. What is wanted in self-education is a correct understanding of our true position and relations—what we are and what we can be. For that Divine Providence who bids us follow the path of the just, which shineth brighter and brighter to the perfect day, would never place one more difficulty in our way than is needed, in order to call forth our slumbering or estranged faculties and powers, and lead us by a faithful co-operation with him, not only to the full development of our whole nature, but to a development and cultivation of that nature which shall render all things healthy and harmonious.

Instead, therefore, of being discouraged, the view which I have presented is, above all others, that which seems to me best calculated to give motive to new exertion and increased activity. The fact that so many difficulties lie in our way, should only serve to urge us onward in the path which leads to certain victory. God made man for himself; but in order to this end he requires that our complicated nature, like his own, should be harmonious. For it is only when man is in peace and harmony with himself that he can be in harmony with his Creator.

And yet once more. The greater the victory to be achieved, the greater the reward. Even the "joy set before" the young man of Nazareth was proportioned to the difficulties which he volunteered to surmount. The more inharmonious your constitutions, taking them as they are in these confines of creation, the higher may you rise, when by faith, and penitence, and patience, and perseverance, you shall have overcome. You are called to achieve victories—one victory at least, the victory over yourself—to which, in all probability, no angel, cherub, or seraph was ever called. Nor is it certain that your upward flight, as I have before said, shall not, in remote periods of eternity, as greatly transcend theirs, as the rejoicings of high heaven over the repenting sinner exceed its rejoicings over the ninety and nine just persons that need no repentance.

To return from this digression—but not at present, as I have written at too great length already. Let me only add, that in future letters, I will endeavor to avoid the preaching style into which, in this communication, I have inadvertently fallen, and pursue a style of instruction—so far as I am capable of instructing—like that which is said to have so much interested the numerous and patient readers of my early work, the "Young Man's Guide"—a work, to which this is intended as a sequel.

LETTER VI.

HARMONY OF CHARACTER.

It has been shown you, in a former letter, that in order to perfection of character, your whole nature, physical, intellectual and moral, must not only be largely developed and cultivated to a high pitch, but must be developed and cultivated in due proportion and harmony. I wish, now, to lead your minds a little farther in the same general direction.

Each of the three great divisions or departments of human nature has also its subdivisions. Thus, what we call the mind, or the intellectual domain, is made up, as you well know, of many different faculties. So the heart, or moral domain, is regarded as including all the various affections and passions.

So, also, the physical department includes brain, nerves, lungs, skin, heart, stomach, &c. &c.

Now it is absolutely necessary, in order to the full and perfect and harmonious development and cultivation of your whole nature, that all these subdivisions of each grand department of humanity should receive its due share of attention. It is, moreover, a physiological truth of high antiquity—that if one member suffers, all the members suffer with it, and that if one member rejoices, all the members rejoice with it! The same law may be applied to the various under-departments of our intellectual and moral nature, no less than to the physical. Whether Paul intended any other application, is, of course, uncertain.*

Permit me, however, to confine your attention for a few moments to the physical depart-

* If the suggestions of Adam Clark, in his Commentary, have weight, there is reason for believing that Paul received a medical education, either at Alexandria or elsewhere. This, alone, would account for his figures of speech.

ment of your nature; and for the sake of illustration to introduce a new figure.

Let us compare the body to a confederacy of smaller States, like the Federal Union in which our lot is cast. Let Massachusetts, if you please, represent the cerebral system; New York, the respiratory or breathing system; Pennsylvania the stomach, and so on; each State representing some important, though by no means equally large and important, organ or system of organs.

Now, can any thing be more obvious than that if the smallest member of this great confederacy suffers—even little Rhode Island—all the other members suffer with it? Or that if one of these members rejoices—has its condition improved—all the others rejoice with it?

And yet it is equally true of the members of the human confederacy of which I have spoken, that they sympathize strongly with each other, and if one rejoices or suffers all the others rejoice or suffer with it. A finger, even, cannot suffer without involving the rest of the system in suffering in some small degree.

One form, in which the suffering to which I

refer is manifested, consists in a want of proper harmony in the system. Thus, if the skin suffers for a considerable time, whether from over-activity or any thing else, the lungs, or some other part which sympathizes strongly with it, is soon thrown off its balance, so to speak, either by being overworked or otherwise.

This, again, produces disturbance in the nervous and digestive systems, and finally a clashing of interests, and perhaps downright opposition. And now a civil war ensues, or may ensue, in which too often the whole confederacy is destroyed. In other instances, however, this inharmonious condition of things constitutes chronic disease of greater or less severity.

Finally, the organs of the body having become involved in war, the evils are extended to the soul and spirit, as Paul calls them; or, in other words, to the intellectual and moral departments of our complicated nature.

This civil war of the human confederacy may be set on foot in a thousand ways. I have no time or room now for detail—hardly for enumeration. Excess or deficiency of their appropriate stimuli; excess of employment, which in these days is too much divided and subdivided; employment which is not well adapted to the constitution and temperament of the individual; unhealthy stimuli applied to the different organs;—these are general names for large classes of causes, which break up or prevent harmony in the physical, and ultimately in the intellectual and moral domain; and, as an indirect but inevitable result, produce a want of proper harmony of character.*

Let me dwell for a moment, in passing, on one point. I have spoken of labor as being too much divided and subdivided, for health and harmony in the physical frame. Do not suppose I am ignorant of the many advantages to be derived from a minute division of labor. Yet all these, important as they may be, are greatly outweighed by the injury done to certain parts of the human system.

* I am not attempting here to teach physiology. This subject and the laws of health I have reserved, chiefly, for another letter and a future volume.

Some of the muscles are overworked; some not worked at all. One organ, or set of organs, for example, is cramped, or its motion impeded; another, having full play, not only does its own work, but attempts to aid its cramped or enfeebled neighbor. Mind, too, in its varied faculties, suffers in a similar way; but this belongs to another department of my subject—to which, by the way, we must now hasten.

In order to insure entire harmony of character, no one of the intellectual faculties should be overtasked or strained on the one hand, or neglected or dwarfed on the other. Yet whether or not you may be conscious of it, this error is committed all the way from the cradle to the grave. The memory is cultivated, it may be, or rather an attempt is made to cultivate it; while perception, attention, comparison and judgment being overlooked or neglected, become enfeebled; and the result is a loss of balance—a want of due harmony—in the mental character. But I have said this before.

Again, in the selection of your studies, the same unwise course is often pursued. Certain studies—say the mathematical ones—receive a large share of your attention, while the others, or some of the others, are neglected. I am greatly pained when I find, as I often do, this great practical error in some of our best schools. On this very point—neglecting the natural sciences and the study of men and things, and substituting in their place, algebra and the languages—harmony of character is daily and hourly destroyed. And the great misfortune of all, concerning it, is, that even our Normal Schools, High Schools, and Colleges, in some instances, are perpetuating the evil.

Conversation, at home and abroad, has very generally the same inharmonious tendency; and so have books. One whole class of school books, in particular, is so constructed—and this without the slightest necessity—as to turn the thoughts, for the most part to money-getting. Public addresses often have the same or worse results. Can the tendency of such things be mistaken, in a country and period like our own? And could any thing be to the young more unfortunate?

But I must not dwell too long on this part of my subject, on account of the pain you will feel at the presentation of so dark a picture. I am even not without fears I shall discourage you. Here we are, you will say, *such* as we are, sufferers in many particulars, both by inheritance and education; and we cannot go back. This I understand, very well. I have been a young man, as well as you. I have felt the difficulties under which you labor—difficulties, however, which are daily and hourly increasing.

And yet—I repeat the sentiment—in order to *get* right and *be* right, you must understand your true position and condition. As well might the wise surgeon dispense with examining—probing, even to the quick—the wounds and ulcers which fall under his observation and care, as the moral physician neglect to begin the work of reformation, in the young, at the foundations of character.

Instead of having gone too far, therefore, I have not yet gone far enough. I have scarcely adverted to the *moral* causes of a want of that harmony in the human character of which I speak. These must not, my young friends, be overlooked; though they may perhaps be deferred for the present.

More than once I have expressed a fear of discouraging you by the magnitude of the work which is assigned you. Yet the beloved apostle calls young men strong, and says he writes to them because they *are* so. And so do I. Of old men—of men above forty, even—I have little hope. But I have great faith in the ability of young men, could that ability be rightly directed.

They are not, I know, quite omnipotent. They cannot wield *mountains* of difficulty with the facility of power which Milton ascribes to the warring angels in his Paradise Lost. And yet they can remove them gradually. And what they can do, as I have already said, they are bound to do.

Nay, there is a sense in which young men, no less than old ones, are bound to do *more than they can.* Their great work (and greater work could not well be assigned them) is victory over themselves—these miseducated, misdirected, inharmonious selves, of which I have been speaking. Yet for this victory even, they are abundantly qualified, because if they go forth to the battle, in the right spirit, the God of Hosts will be with them; and what power they cannot command of themselves, as young men merely, his abundant favor will supply.

LETTER VII.

SELF-INSTRUCTION.

It will require a long time to free the minds of young men from the erroneous impression that their education is completed in the schools; whereas the instruction of these institutions, important as it is, should merely present us with the *keys* of knowledge. To obtain these, is a comparatively trifling work; to unlock the golden treasures to which they give us access, is the work of a life. Education, in its largest sense, as we have already seen, is a life work. Even that part of education which we call instruction, only *begins* in the schools; at least, it should be so. With too many, it both begins and ends there.

I have sometimes wondered why it is, that

in a country which has produced a Franklin, and where so many young men have superior advantages to those which that philosopher, while young, enjoyed, we have so few Franklins. Is it not because so few continue, as he did, to old age, the work of self-instruction?

The road to eminence which Franklin trod, is as surely open as the road to wealth, or political distinction. As well may the young man take Franklin for his model as John Jacob Astor, or Stephen Girard; nay, even as Washington or Napoleon.

The desire for improvement in our American young men, is most certainly feeble—I mean as a general rule. I do not forget, now, the tendency of old men to place the golden age in the past. We have facts. Meursius, an ancient writer, has shown that there were, in his time, "more than three hundred public places in Athens" alone, to which "the principal youth and reputable citizens were accustomed to resort for the purpose of conversation and inquiry." And we have the testimony of Luke, the companion of Paul, that the Athenians were a thinking people—spending much of their time in the pursuit of knowledge of some sort.

Shall the young men of the United States of America, in 1849, be behind the young men of heathen Athens of 54? And yet have we not great reason to fear they are so? One tenth the number of institutions for mutual improvement, in the same population, would, in these days, be a novel sight.

Of course, I do not mean to say that there are no exceptions to the truth of these remarks, for there are many—some of them honorable ones. Even in those parts of the country where no school instruction has hitherto been enjoyed, the young man has occasionally "started out of the ranks," and made himself eminent, at least among his fellows.

I knew a man, not long since—then about fourscore—who, without the opportunity of attending school for a single day during his whole life, had become quite distinguished in his own neighborhood. And how was this distinction attained? Was it without effort—patient, persevering effort? Never.

This man, in early life, having been taught

by his mother to read a little, laid by money, and purchased a dictionary. It was by no means a large or costly work; but then it was precious to him. Whenever, in reading or conversation, he encountered a hard word, he examined his dictionary, found the meaning, and retained it.

This laid the foundation of a good mind; and indeed of a large fund of what the philosopher Locke used to call large, sound, roundabout common sense. Now what this plain, obscure individual could do, others, in circumstances a thousand times more favor able, most certainly can.

I have in my mind's eye, at this moment, another young man, who without either dictionary or school, for the first years of his life, availed himself of every advantage, which the family in which he resided afforded him, and became, at length, quite a respectable scholar. He was at eighteen a schoolmaster; and at twenty-five, at the summit of this profession.

Is it for want of time that more is not done? Who has not as much time as Franklin had? Who has not as much of this precious commodity, to say the least, as the man of whom I have been speaking? Is it for want of money? Who has not money enough to buy a dictionary? Every young man has shreds, both of time and money, which might be saved for this purpose.*

Young men, however, are very far from being driven to as close quarters as all this would imply. They can have more than a dictionary. Most of them have newspapers; bad, good, or indifferent. And much may be learned from any of these—even the worst. Man's mental stomach, like his physical, is made susceptible of receiving and procuring nourishment from almost every kind of food.

Then, again, few families can be found, in which a young man could be thrown, who

* I can hardly forbear, in this place, to commend to young men, the beautiful edition of Noah Webster's Dictionary, unabridged, lately published. It is one of the noblest productions of our language; and is of itself a library. What would the dictionary man above mentioned have thought of such a treasure? What would Franklin? Two cents a day—and this many young men might save in cigars or coffee—in one year, would more than procure it.

have not more or fewer books; some of them valuable ones. Besides this, there are circulating, parish and school libraries. And lastly, there are lyceums, clubs, debating societies, &c., of whose advantages most young men may avail themselves, or, if there are not enough of these, more may be established.

One or two errors in reading, and indeed in self-instruction generally, remain to be noticed. Not a few young men fall into the error of reading too much. This is especially the case with those who use no dictionary. They who make it a point to understand every thing they read, and who constantly ask the meaning of new words, terms and phrases which obstruct their course, will not be likely to fall into the wretched habit which is often alluded to by saying that it passes into one ear and out at the other. They will do something more than merely devour books—swallow them whole—they will "read, mark, learn, and inwardly digest."

Another error consists in sitting up to read late at night. I speak not here of the physical dangers, great as they are; but rather of the mental and moral dangers of this practice. It is greatly unfavorable to the growth of mind —to its healthy growth especially. But I think it still more unfavorable to moral growth and progress.

Do you ask why it is so? There are many and various reasons. One is, that what is read at a late hour, when we are over-fatigued in body and mind, being usually of an exciting character, only tends to fill the brain with unnatural images, during both our waking and sleeping hours. Fancy and imagination are apt to predominate, at this hour of the day, and sober judgment seldom gains the ascendency. If exciting books are read at all, they should be read in the forenoon, and not in the evening. Should it be said that other books might be read at these late hours, as well as the class I have described, my reply is, they will not be, as a general fact. The appetite at this hour as seldom craves such food for the mind as for the body.

LETTER VIII.

LIGHT READING.

So numerous are the influences which have an unfavorable tendency on young men, by forming inharmonious and therefore unhappy character, that one hardly knows at what point to commence his remarks. I propose, however, to bring before your minds, at the present time, the subject of LIGHT READING, the topic with which I closed my last letter.

But I must define my terms; for one-half the mental confusion—not to say mischief of this world—has its origin in vague or undefined words and terms. By light reading, then, I mean such books, papers and periodicals as amuse and enable you to "kill time," or at least "while" it away; but leave little or no lasting impression on the mind and heart.—Among these, stand conspicuous many of our more popular periodicals.

In a former letter, I alluded to the evils of a minute division of labor. One would think that such division would save time for other purposes, such as reading and study—and this, I confess, is its natural tendency. Yet such is the operation of various circumstances and influences, that people seem not only to have less time for other purposes than formerly, but also less disposition to make a wise and profitable use of their leisure hours, whenever they arrive.

The mania for light reading, which has been more or less prevalent ever since the adventures of Paul on Mars Hill, has of late been increasing. We not only confine ourselves more than formerly to light reading, but we read still more "by snatches!"

For this ever-increasing but ever-unfavorable habit, the present age furnishes almost unbounded facilities. There never was a time when so many books and newspapers were circulated as at the present day.

Then, again, they are exceedingly cheap. Few families can be found who do not take one or more newspapers or magazines; and not a few take three or four, including at least *one* daily. Some, indeed, there are who take from five to ten or twelve continually. One family I visited lately—that of a mechanic—takes fourteen. Another family I know takes about a dozen.

I will not stop here to caution you against receiving this or that paper, or journal, or magazine; or to commend to your favorable regard the other. To this and other particulars, I may or may not descend by and by. What I propose, at this time, is to dissuade you, if possible, from your present course; and suggest one which is not only more favorable to a healthful and harmonious growth of character, but actually more pleasurable in the passing moment

The more you read mere fragments, the more you are inclined to do so; and the more you will disrelish any and every other mode. And the more you spend your shreds of time in this way, on the plea that they are *mere* shreds. the shorter they seem to become. This, at least, is the result of my own observation—nor has my opportunity or range for observation been very limited.

This will probably explain the well-known fact that light reading, and reading little more than mere shreds—such as abound in the papers, especially the dailies—is perpetually increasing, so that no one can tell where it is likely to end.

I am no enemy, by the way, to light reading. Books, magazines, and newspapers of this sort, all have their place. A small share of our time, however valuable this precious gift of God may be—and no one, I am sure, can estimate it too highly—may be very properly expended on some kinds of light reading. But so long as human nature remains as it now is—perhaps as long as it exists—the tendency to excess will need to be watched and guarded against. Few, if any, read light works too little.

Some six or seven months ago, I was stopping for a short time in one of the flourishing villages of New England, when two individuals came through the street selling books. One had such works as The Young Man's Guide, The Young Mother, Young Wife, &c. The other had books of a very different character—and among the rest, the catchpennies of the day, such as the cheaper lives of Scott, Taylor, the works of Eugene Sue, &c. The latter sold readily—the former hardly at all.

Now I will not take it upon me to commend the former or condemn the latter, by wholesale; but I am justified in condemning that public taste which wholly excludes the plain and practical, and seizes and devours indiscriminately the noisy, the light, or the visionary; and yet nothing can be more certain than that such are the tendencies of things at the present time.

If this state of things is to continue for half a century to come—if the young mind, I mean, is to go on in its present course, becoming more and more averse to any thing solid, and more and more inclined to light papers, and novels, and catchpennies, it is quite difficult to predict the final issue of things. Certain it is, however, that they can be only evil, and that continually.

Against this depraved taste, and these depraved mental habits, my young friends, let me most earnestly entreat you to enter your protest. If life were *long* enough to read *every thing*, not every thing the press pours forth would be fit for you to read. And if you can justify yourselves in reading one hour a day, or so, the lighter works—those in which fancy and not fact predominate—how can you allow yourselves in devoting your days and nights to them? And if you are willing to glance at a daily paper—the common catchpenny dailies, I mean, and not the more respectable ones—now and then, does it follow that you are doing right when you spend an hour or two on them of every day you live?

What I have said thus far, in this letter, has been said on the supposition that these "light concerns," were only negatively injurious; that is, that they only injure you, by frittering away your time, and feeding a distempered taste and brain.

But I have more to say against them. Not

a few are positively injurious—first, by the false colorings they hold out, and the false views they present of human life; secondly, by the depravity and infidelity which, under a mistaken garb, they too often conceal; thirdly, by the downright falsities which some of them contain.

The more you find yourself inclined to read by snatches, and to prefer light books and periodicals to those which are more solid, the more active should be your organ of caution. "I tremble for the man who does not tremble for himself," said an aged advocate of teetotalism; and I can adopt his language in relation to the subject before you. A young man who trembles for himself is the only young man who is safe. *He* may possibly be cautious how he ventures beyond his ken or depth in waters unknown to him; no one else I am sure will be.

If there were no books, papers or magazines among us, which in their character approximate to what they should be, the case would be greatly altered. But that state of civilized society which brings upon us a flood of light papers and magazines, and a world of mawkish and sickly stuff, whose only recommendation is that it is new and cheap, brings us at the same time many highly valuable publications, both new and old, and at a greatly reduced price. He must be poor, indeed, who has his health, if he cannot procure a library of choice reading, both periodical and permanent.

Those of us who complain of the present state of things, in the gross, should not fail to remember that there never was a time before, when so much choice reading could be procured for so little money. And we should not only remember the fact, but be grateful.

He who would educate himself in the best possible manner, and who would stand before the community not only in harmony with his Creator, but also with himself, should be more careful in the choice of his books and papers than in the choice of any thing else in the wide world, except friends. Indeed, books and papers—materials for reading and thinking—*are* friends. Happy, then, the young man who is so fortunate as to make a wise selection!

Young men are usually fond of history and biography—and they ought to be. They love to study men and things. Would they were as anxious to know *themselves* as to become acquainted with *others;* for then, should they catch the spirit of reform, they might, perchance, be as anxious to mend themselves as to point out to others the path of amendment, or sneer at their imperfections.

This love of studying men and things, I have said, is laudable. It is only a morbid desire of this kind that leads the young to search the outside pages of newspapers, and the inside of magazines and works of fiction, for something wherewith to feed what *might* have been fanned into a heavenly flame. It is this never-satisfied and never-to-be-satisfied desire that furnishes a market for certain papers which I couid name, by thousands and tens of thousands, while not a few of our more meritorious ones hardly pay their way.

I grant, indeed, that the details of real life are sometimes more wonderful, as well as more inviting, than romance. But this is not usually so. The better histories of the better class of mankind are not in general spiced high enough for those who have not been trained to plain food. Oberlin and Howard are read with far less interest than Napoleon and Alexander; and Jesus Christ and his apostles with still less than either.

Be exhorted, then, to correct a false taste as soon as possible. Accustom yourselves to read a portion of biography or history, sacred or profane, every day you live. The more you read, in this way, just as it is with plain food for the body, the more you will find yourselves satisfied with plain things, and the less will you be disposed to read that to which I have been all along objecting; and above all, of that which can never profit you, but must only perish in the using.

Read, too, as you may have opportunity, the lives of distinguished reformers. Our Saviour was indeed the greatest of them; and to his life and deeds, I have already directed your attention. But I have also to direct you to the lives of some of his followers.

I begin with Paul. Let me be understood here. I am not speaking now so much in the character of a religious man, as that of an educationist. Would you educate yourselves, learn much more than you have ever yet learned of Paul.

Then, to come to later times, study Luther. For this purpose, perhaps, you will do well to procure D'Aubigné's History of the Reformation. Luther was not faultless; but you may learn much from him about self-education to virtuous and energetic character.

Howard and Oberlin come next, in my estimation. You will be most pleased, I think, however, with the latter. Perhaps he was not so great a man as the former; but then he was quite as practical.

In later times, still, there are many bright, shining examples, among the modern missionaries. Here I will not particularize, for obvious reasons. But I know not where you can go, among the living, for such specimens of all that is truly great and noble, as among these very men.

Take, for example, a case cited by Sir Gilbert

Blane, in his Medical Jurisprudence. Anxious to save time, that he might complete the translation of an important work, the missionary contrived, or at least endeavored to contract his sleep into very narrow space. He would go to sleep in his chair, holding a little ball over a tin basin or bell; and as soon as he was fairly asleep the ball would drop, and the sound would wake him. A few such naps, as he believed, answered his purpose, and thus he seemed to save half his night for study.

This last case, I do not recommend to you as an example; but it shows to what a pitch this moral heroism is sometimes carried. It shows you, too, that time redeemed, is *worth* something.

LETTER IX.

CORRECT CONVERSATION.

One means of self-education—a most important means, too—is conversation. Indeed, the art of conversing correctly should be always made a part of the education of our families and our schools. It is of a thousand times more consequence than some of the subjects which are made so prominent there, especially during the earlier years of life.

How many of you were drilled, for example, every day, or nearly every day of your school education, for months and years, in what is commonly called English Grammar! And to what purpose? Were you made either wiser or better for it? Was it not, to you, a sort of confusion, rather than any thing which justly deserves the name of real knowledge? Were you not, in truth, disgusted with it?

Some of you, who have in your turn become teachers, may have found use for it, when it became necessary that, in order to please parents and comply with fashion, you must teach the same unintelligible jargon to your own pupils. I do not say that even this use is to be commended. I only speak of it as a commodity, for which now-a-days there is a market.

Suppose, that the same amount of time which is spent on "grammar" were spent on conversation. English Grammar is said to be the art of speaking and writing our language correctly. But in order to *write* the language correctly, we should first know how to *speak* it correctly. What is correct writing, or good composition, but good conversation transferred to paper?

From the first moment you began to talk, all the way through your family and school education, care should have been taken to have you *talk right*. Force, distinctness, clearness, propriety—all, in truth, that makes conversation answer best the designs of the Creator—should have been attended to most assiduously. There should have been no mumbling, no confusion, no hesitancy, no repetition, no unmeaning words or phrases, no vulgarisms, and no double negatives.

Has this been your lot? If so, that lot has been singularly happy. Nine in ten of our youth of both sexes—I might say, as I have reason to fear, nineteen-twentieths—receive a very different treatment. They are spoiled from the first in the family, and what is "bred in the bone," as the vulgar saying is, "stays long in the flesh." The schools do not correct the error.

It is surprising what an amount of ungrammatical stuff is tolerated among us. "I han't got no book;" or "I can't get so long a lesson, I don't think;" or "Please, sir, John is a pinchin' on me;" or other equally incorrect and ungrammatical expressions, are carried through the schools—grammar, as it is called, both English and Latin, to the contrary notwithstanding.

Now let me entreat those who read this

letter, and who, though pronounced grammarians by the constituted authorities, yet "murder the King's English" at every step they take, to reflect on the predicament in which they have been placed, and resolve at once to escape it. The task is not so difficult as they may at first suppose—the greatest difficulty is in resolving and beginning.

But you will hardly emancipate yourselves alone. Do not undertake the work, therefore, single-handed. Call to your aid some kind friend—one, it may happen, who himself needs the same sort of discipline, and who in teaching may learn, and in giving retain. A brother, or a sister, or even a neighbor or a schoolfellow, will serve your purpose very well. Or, perhaps, you may draft to your aid two or three. The more, the better, provided they work in the right spirit.

She whom you choose as a companion for life will be a more efficient helper in the work than any other individual—but alas! her assistance often comes late. The work of reformation, in this particular, ought to be completed long before you enter into the matrimonial relation.

One means of correct conversation consists in teaching others to speak correctly. Some little child, in whose society you find yourself, will need to be set right from day to day; and nothing will have a better effect to confirm, in you, good habits, than endeavoring to confirm them in a child. You thus learn from happy experience the truth of the saying, He that watereth shall himself be watered.

Another useful practice is to write out a list, from day to day, of those incorrect words and phrases which you are most anxious to avoid. You will be surprised, no doubt, at the largeness of the list; and perhaps, at times, feel discouraged. But never give up the contest; for you will overcome, at length, if you faint not.

Let me not be understood as objecting wholly to the study of English Grammar; for there is a way and a time for this branch. What is wanted, however, in early life, is correct conversation; a style of conversation from mere habit that is exactly in accordance with the rules of the language. And then, at a somewhat later period of your school studies, a course of lessons on the philosophy of that language which you have already learned to speak and write correctly from mere habit, may be useful.

It has long been a fundamental maxim with grammarians, that they who are learning to compose their sentences with accuracy and order, are learning at the same time to *think* with accuracy and order. But it is also true, and in a degree still more striking, that they who are learning to speak correctly, are at the same time learning to compose accurately.

But I will not dwell on this topic too long; for it is one of the plainest things in the world, that correct conversation is grammatical; and that correct or grammatical conversation from the cradle upward, in all the circumstances of recreation or employment in which we are placed, would insure correct composition.

Let the work of correct conversation, then, begin where it ought. Let it begin, moreover, immediately. Let us not speak incorrectly at home, and elsewhere, all our early years, and then expect a few lessons, or a few days at the school, will set all right.

LETTER X.

THE SCHOOLS.

SOME among you, after reading my last letter, may be ready to infer that I am unfriendly to the schools. Nothing, however, could be more incorrect than such an inference.

For though I am not much indebted to them, at least directly, yet I doubt whether you can find one man in a thousand who thinks more highly of them than I do. Besides teaching about ten years, lecturing to thousands of them on physiology, &c., I have probably visited more schools in the United States than any other individual. And I still visit them—for the mere love I bear them. It is but a short time since I visited nine of them in a single day

But to value the schools highly, in view of what they *might* accomplish, is one thing—to be *satisfied* with them, quite another. For saying nothing more about the stupidity of studying English Grammar for months and years to no purpose, or to a purpose worse than none, I am quite disgusted with the common practice of dabbling with almost every thing—i. e. with the elements of almost every thing—and being thorough in nothing.

Were it so that we could have these schools what they ought to be—what they must one day become—places where every individual might obtain, free of any direct tax, the elements or keys of all that is indispensable to a thorough English education, and at the same time have hours enough each day for labor and study, I should be as strong a friend of schools as any other individual. Indeed, to repeat what I have already said, I value them now, with all their defects; especially when I think what they may, and will, and must become.

But in order to derive the greatest possible advantage from these schools, your time should not be spent in learning to read, at random, the thoughts of others to which your minds are not yet adequate; nor in special lessons daily in writing, composition, &c. You should make your own reading lessons for several of the first of your school years. These reading lessons will, at the same time, form your best compositions, to which, however, should be added letter-writing, and keeping a journal. And in doing all this, you will not fail to learn to write.

There is little difficulty in making your own sentences, written on your slates or black boards, form at the same time your principal lessons—and this for years—in spelling, defining, reading, writing, arithmetic, grammar, geography, and history. Two years spent in this way, would give the *keys* of learning; which is all that is usually got in ten years. With the keys in your hands, and with suitable books and teachers, you might now obtain, in the common schools, all that is valuable in our best university education—except, perhaps, that which pertains exclusively to what are called the learned professions. It is down-

right folly to be ten, twelve, or fourteen years, in trying to get hold of the keys, and then never getting them. It reminds one too much of the condition of old Tantalus.

But do not be impatient because you cannot do all you wish in these schools. They are essentially republican in their structure. Here meet together—if not now, it will ere long be so—the high and the low, the rich and the poor, the bond and the free. Here they are educated, or at least instructed, not as lords and vassals, but as brethren.

These schools, however, would be worth much more, as republican institutions, if they were places of *education* as well as of *instruction.* To give our citizens, as a mass, the mere keys of learning, though a good thing, comes far enough short of what is needed. Is not the body worthy of some good degree of attention as well as the mind? Why should not the schools give us the keys of health as well as of science? Is the latter of so much value, and the former hardly worth a lesson, or even a thought?

And why not, too, the keys of virtue and

purity, as well as of knowledge and health? Is it nothing to be good, and virtuous, and happy? What good purpose would it answer to give a whole generation the keys of health and knowledge, and set them to using them, while they were made no better able nor any more disposed to unlock and use the still more —I was going to say *infinitely* more—valuable treasures to fallen man—morality and religion? Would Satan be made better and happier, simply by being made wiser and healthier? Would he not be made, by just so much as he was made to know more, only the more truly and completely devil?

How strange it is that the schools—with few exceptions—have done little more than to teach the young to find their level in a society which is theoretically republican, and which ought to be so practically! I do most ardently desire to live till the blessed day shall arrive, when the young will be taught, in all our schools, from the highest to the lowest, the essentials of that which will make them, at once, healthier, wiser, and better!

There are a thousand little habits of conduct

and conversation which should be taught the young at school, which, weighed in the true balances, would be found far more valuable in their bearing on life and life's great ends, than mere book-knowledge. The time will come, sooner or later, when the schools will teach all this.

Till that time, I say once more, have a little patience; but, then, do not be inactive. You may by your own effort, as a pupil in the schools, or afterward as teacher or proprietor, do much to hasten that glad day. So that if the schools cannot be, in your own time, what you desire, they may be so in your children's day—or in that of your children's children. For you live for the race, or should do so, no less than for yourselves as individuals.

LETTER XI.

THE LOVE AND SPIRIT OF PROGRESS.

Is it thought that the views I have presented, when writing on self-dependence and self-education, do not quite harmonize with those of my last letter? That at one time, I teach the young man that his great business is to educate himself, and at another, that the schools are useful as a means of educating him—both of which cannot be true?

Now I do not think there is any discrepancy of the kind to be found in my letters. I have not said, either in one place or another, that we cannot be educated,—nay, even *instructed*—without the aid of the schools. Neither have I said that the schools might not be made to assist us—not by *educating* us, so much, as by giving us the means of educating ourselves. The latter they most certainly might do for us; and I trust one day will. This is about *all* they can profitably do; though even this is not to be despised.

After all, it is not the schools that are to make us what we ought to be—nor is it any array of means or machinery, whether of human or divine ordination. If a young man intends to be any thing in this world, he must possess, somehow or other, *the love of improvement*—and a zeal as strong as his love. He must "hunger and thirst" to make progress.

He must not only desire, generally, to become wiser and better, but he must embody this desire, as it were, by carrying it into particulars. Many hunger and thirst enough; but take no such measures as they ought, to allay their hunger, or slake their thirst. They resolve, it may be, and re-resolve, and yet go on, (and even go on till they die,) of the same character they always have been.

Now such persons must cease to deal so much in generals—never coming to particulars. They are like the theoretically benevolent, who are always mourning over a world's miseries in general, but never doing any thing, in particular, to relieve them. They must become practical penitents, or their penitence will be of little avail.

For example, when they rise in the morning, they must make resolutions and lay plans, not for life in general, and somewhere, and at some time or other, but for that day specifically. The question should be, What ought I to do, that is practical, in the way of self-improvement, *to-day?* And this question being settled, good resolutions should immediately follow. And good resolutions being made, they should be lived up to. Or, finally, if not lived up to, we should be as in sackcloth and ashes on account of it.

I have spoken of the schools and of self-education. Now give me but the love of progress—the desire of improvement—the never-ending hunger and thirst after righteousness—and it matters but little about the schools. What schools they are; where they are; what their forms or methods; how long we attend them—these are all things of comparatively little importance. They may have their use—they do have it; they serve to feed in us the heaven-like flame, instead of quenching it. And this, to express again, though in different words, the same idea, is their legitimate office.

I have seen scores of people who hungered and thirsted after more knowledge, and who contrived to bring much of it within their grasp. I knew a female, who, though mistress of a large family and intensely occupied in taking the sole charge of them, contrived to slake her thirst and appease her hunger for books. No female I ever knew worked harder; and yet few whom I have known ever read more. And it was read to good purpose. It was understood and remembered. It was even more than this; it was *marked, learned, and inwardly digested.*

And yet I sometimes doubted—for I knew well the circumstances—whether this female was made a whit the better for all this. A boy of ten years of age, of the same habits, seemed none the better for it, but the worse. Both loved to become wiser; both, perhaps, had a feeble, half formed desire to become better; but still nothing was done to effect what was but faintly desired.

It has been partially admitted that there are many among us—some scores at least—who desire to become wiser, though they do not give evidence that they care to become better. But I recall. From all I can learn in the case, they are seeking—hungering and thirsting for—mere gratification, with as little thought or care whether it will or will not make them any better, as those persons have who are eating and drinking what tickles their appetite and satisfies the cravings, or at least the gnawings, of their stomachs. Can we say, in these circumstances, that they give evidence of a love of progress or desire for improvement?

He who has that most excellent trait of character of which I am now speaking, is not only solicitous to have every thing he says and does have a good effect upon him, physically and morally, but, at times, painfully suspicious lest they should have the contrary effect. He might, in many a reflecting moment, adopt the soliloquy of Mr. Burgh, in his "Dignity of Human Nature:"

"Dost thou, Oh my soul, constantly watch over thyself? Dost thou suspect every other person, lest his example, or influence, mislead thee? Dost thou often and regularly meditate on thy ways, and examine thy heart and life? Dost thou perfectly know thy own weakness? Hast thou all thy infirmities engraven on thy remembrance? Dost thou habitually labor to make sure of keeping within bounds? Dost thou often deny thyself rather than run the smallest hazard of offending?"

I would give more for the love of progress in son or daughter, than for almost any merely intellectual or moral qualification below the sun. It is a trait of character which is the more valuable from the fact that it so well becomes creatures like ourselves—expressly made for it. We do not know that angels and seraphs are constructed, in their natures, on the same plan. But ourselves we know better—over ourselves we have control; so God has ordered it.

See, then, that you possess the quality to which I have alluded in these paragraphs.

Of whatever else you may be deprived, lose not the golden treasure of a true hungering and thirsting after improvement in knowledge and piety. Let your path, in every important respect, be that of the just, which shineth brighter and brighter unto the perfect day.

LETTER XII.

LOVE OF INQUIRY, OR FREE-THINKING.

It is too late in the day of human progress—the progress, I mean, of the race—to exhort young men to shun free inquiry and free-thinking. In truth, it is a piece of advice which in any age of the world, above all in our own, I should have no disposition to give. Both these, on the contrary, I would encourage.

There is, however, a slight difference between the two, as may be seen by a moment's reflection. Free inquiry would lead us to investigate, unshackled, any subject, which in itself is worthy of our attention. Free-thinking may or may not be disposed to make inquiry. It only assumes the right of forming unbiased opinions on all subjects that come before the mind's eye, whether they be few or many; and whether they are forced upon it—the mind itself being passive—or are dug out, like the gold of California.

I have said that to neither of these I had any sort of objection; and more than this, that I would encourage both. And I most ardently desire that every young man, as soon as he thinks at all, will be in the highest and most important sense of the word, a free-thinker.

It is a low and partial view of this subject that leaves an impression on the minds of some of our older or middle-aged people, that free-thinking is synonymous with skcpticism; that a man who thinks freely, especially a person who is young and inexperienced, must almost of necessity think *wrong*, &c. Such a view, besides being low, seems to me an impeachment of the wisdom and goodness of God. For as he most obviously created man to *think*, and in every age has *required* him to think, to assume that in thinking freely he will almost inevitably think wrong—is it not akin to blasphemy? At least, is it not irreverent?

That not a few free-thinkers have become skeptical. is admitted. But that free-thinking in its *own* nature, tends to skepticism, can never be true. Bacon, indeed, says that "a little knowledge inclineth man's mind to atheism; but depth in knowledge bringeth it about to true religion." But then there are two things to be considered here; first, that atheism is not exactly synonymous with skepticism; and secondly, that the little knowledge of which he speaks is not the knowledge of the *free-thinker*, but of him who *does not* think freely.

Greatly do I rejoice when I find a young man who *thinks*, even if his road should chance to lead through skepticism. I found a boy the other day, scarcely six years of age, who was constantly thinking and inquiring. Nothing came before his eye which did not excite his most earnest attention, and lead him to his father. What is this for, father? he would say. And what is that? And the answers to the first inquiries would lead to others, sometimes almost innumerable.

Such a father may think his case a hard

one, and it may be so to him who does not understand the matter. It may even be thought a heavy tax upon his time. To me, however, such taxation would be no tyranny. On the contrary, I should rejoice that God had given me an inquisitive son. He might, for aught I should know, become a skeptic ; but I should hope better things. I should hope that depth in knowledge would bring him about to true religion in the end. And of one thing I should be certain, viz : that if he ever came to true religion, he would not be a superficial, but a *thorough* Christian.

Fear not, then, to indulge in freedom of thinking ; and to love and practise free inquiry. To do this is your natural and inalienable right—born, as you are, a republican and not a monarchist—a Christian, and not a Turk or a Pagan. It is guarantied you by the constitution of the country you live in ; it is guarantied you by the principles of Protestantism ; it is guarantied you by God himself.

In regard to the requirements of Protestantism in this matter, allow me to quote from the farewell discourse or address of Rev. Mr. Robinson to the Pilgrims, as they have been called —I mean the emigrants from Europe who first settled New England.

"I charge you before God and his blessed angels, that you follow me no farther than you have seen me follow the Lord Jesus Christ. The Lord has more truth yet to break forth out of his Holy Word. I cannot sufficiently bewail the condition of the reformed churches who are come to a period in their religion. I will go at present no farther than the instruments of their reformation. Luther and Calvin were great and shining lights in their times, yet they penetrated not into the whole counsel of God. I beseech you remember it, 'tis an article of your church covenant, that you be ready to receive whatever truth shall be made known to you from the written word of God."

This is the voice of a free-thinker—a friend of free inquiry—a man who in all ages will be deemed a great man, because he thought and inquired, freely and gave it in charge to others, even as friends of religion and religious truth, to do the same. Here was no fear of skepticism, open or covert. My own belief is—and such I doubt not has been the belief of many a man of thought and inquiry, John Robinson among the rest—that there is no such effectual antidote to licentiousness and skepticism in these matters, as true free-thinking, and true free inquiry.

Still it would be the height of weakness in me or any other individual, to take the ground which some have taken, that what is most wanted in society is to have men—young and old—be induced to think. Now I acknowledge there is not *much thought in the world.* I wish as much as any man there were more. But then, another thing is more needed among us—*much* more—viz: *thinking right.* And superadded to both these, as their crowning glory, should be another thing still, viz: *feeling right. Feeling*, I grant, is blind; but then, when guided by reason, is of inestimable importance.

This may be the proper place to say a little more distinctly than I have yet done, that I would never encourage the society of either books or men, who under the pretence of free inquiry, would lead you to sneer at every thing which is established, merely *because* it is established. Opinions in religion, politics, philosophy, &c., are not *necessarily* erroneous, because established.

In my boyhood, I took up one day, for perusal, one of the volumes of Thomas Paine. He was, as you know, not only a free-thinker, but a skeptic. I was, moreover, of the same turn and tendency. Many of his thoughts on politics, I had long before read and imbibed. But here he was assailing Christianity. Having read a few pages, I threw aside the book in disgust. I had looked for *free*-thinking, instead of which I found *no* thinking. The veriest child who had read the New Testament might have seen it.

I wondered, when I reflected on the subject, how so many could be enamored of the writings of Paine—a man who, though possessed of much intellectual power, would nevertheless stoop to sneer at what he had, most certainly, never examined. If this volume is a fair specimen of the *man*, it is not to be wondered at that while he has so many followers in politics, he has so few in religion.

While, therefore, I counsel you to be men of free inquiry, I wish you to understand, most distinctly, that there is a sort of pseudo free inquiry abroad, which I would have you avoid. It will do you no good; it will be a waste of your time as well as energy. Life is long enough for free inquiry; but not long enough for sneering, or even for trifling.

LETTER XIII.

THE RIGHT USE OF OURSELVES.

MUCH is said, in these days—something has been said even in my former letters—about the importance, to the young especially, of studying themselves. "Know thyself," we have been told, is a maxim of thousands of years' standing; and yet, a maxim which passes almost wholly unheeded. Even the knowledge of our physical frames—their structure, laws and relations; or, in other words, Anatomy, Physiology, and Hygiene—is one of the last things, as I have shown, which young men study, or are required to study. Greek, Latin, Mathematics, &c., are permitted to occupy their attention, to the exclusion of this species of self-knowledge.

And this complaint, when it does not arise from mere querulousness, or from that species of old age which ever complains of the present, while it places the golden age always in the past, is not without just foundation. We know something, or at least attempt to know something, of every body else—noble or ignoble, affluent or indigent, bond or free, colored or white. We know something, as we have seen, of the three kingdoms of nature, all except ourselves.

We explore continent, island, ocean, air. We dig deep the bowels of the earth, and soar among clouds, if not stars. Nay, we even survey, by the aid of the telescope, other worlds; and if we do not become omnipresent or omniscient, we seem to be almost so. Yet after all, we come back to the "house we live in," utterly ignorant of its structure, laws or relations—ten to one if we are not ignorant of the number of its apartments, or the nature and character of its furniture.

Of our minds, too, we are almost as ignorant as of our bodies. Nor do the schools—though they may do much—ever take up this subject, as it ought to be taken up. Nor do reformers of society—the physiological reformers perhaps excepted—ever dwell very much on this great subject.

Something, then, being obviously wrong, what is to be done? On this topic I shall endeavor to dwell, at greater length, in my next letter —that on Physiology. We will dismiss this part of our subject, then, for the present.

There is one thing of which we are still more ignorant than of ourselves, viz. the *right use* of ourselves. Of this ignorance, one author at least—Mudie, in his "Observation of Nature,"—has taken notice. How little know we of the right use of ourselves, as a whole! And how much less of the right use of the various parts composing the whole!

Man, I have said, is made up, as Paul expresses it, of body, head, and heart; or, as the moderns have it, of a physical, an intellectual, and a moral nature. Is the right use of each of these grand divisions of humanity well understood?

Man is made, in the moral department, for example, to do good. Has the science of doing good—the science of benevolence, or rather of philanthropy—been much studied? And does a young man understand, rightly, the use of himself, who does not understand this noble science?

But leaving these grand divisions of ourselves, let us be a little more particular. The physical part of our being, like our moral and intellectual, has its various subdivisions. Thus we have many and different systems, as they are called, united, as we have before seen, under one federal head. We have the nervous system, the circulatory system, the digestive system, the respiratory system, &c. Then, again, we have the five senses, hearing, seeing, tasting, smelling and feeling. And once more, still, we have head, body, hands, feet, &c.

Take the hand. Who is there among us that knows, to the full extent, the right use of this little organ? I do not mean to ask, who knows the *extent* to which its powers may be developed and cultivated, for this would be too broad a topic for discussion here; but merely the uses to which the Creator intended it should be applied.

How far it should be used in the arts, how far in manufactures, how far in the daily customs and personal habits of life, and when and where machinery ought to be substituted, are questions which have seldom been asked. The Germans have a proverb, "Never touch your eye, except with your elbow." The interdict might be extended to the ear, the nostrils, the mouth, &c. Do you say that these are small matters?—Granted; but "who hath despised the day of small things?" Or, if they are to be despised or overlooked, as matters of fact, they may at least serve the purpose of illustration.

Take, again, the human lungs. Remarks concerning these will not surely be regarded as small matters. What, then, is their use? or, rather, what are their uses? First, they aid in forming the blood. The chyle is not fully changed into the former fluid, till it has passed into the lungs, and been spread over the surface of those air bladders, or small hollow cells, of which the lungs are so largely made up. Secondly, the lungs are the chief organ for purifying the blood, after it has become partly spoiled in its ordinary circulation. Thirdly, they are the great fireplace of the "house we live in;" or, in other words, they are the principal caloric agent of the human system.

But I will not enlarge. These illustrations must suffice. No higher subject can be presented to young men than the right use of themselves; especially when we affix to this phrase the highest and truest definition. For will it not include the whole circle of human duty—to ourselves, the world, and God?

I grant, indeed, that merely to *know* the right use of ourselves is not all. To *use* ourselves according to the Divine intention, is of greater importance still. Would that young men understood the right use of themselves in all respects, and would govern themselves accordingly. For as is the young man, individually or collectively, so is the old; so, even, is society.

Were the young to use themselves rightly through half a dozen generations—were they to make the same untiring effort to answer the great Creator's purposes throughout, that they now do to elevate themselves without regard to duty, the world would once more become as Eden, and the desert rejoice and blossom as the rose.

I must here urge on you the study of the great laws of health and life, as developed by the science of Anatomy, Physiology, and Hygiene. Few things are more interesting, when the subject is made intelligible, and fewer still are more important. In another letter, I will throw out a few hints on this great subject. Not that I shall attempt to teach largely this great threefold science, but only show that it should be taught, and endeavor to inspire you with the desire to be made acquainted with it. For to create the desire, is to go full half way in accomplishing it.

LETTER XIV.

PHYSIOLOGY.

By Physiology, in the popular acceptation of that term, is meant all such knowledge as pertains to the physical education and management of human beings. It is in this sense that I use it, when I commend the science to your favorable notice and regard.

The study of man—the physical department, I mean, of this great science—is usually divided, as I told you in my last letter, into three great branches. First, Anatomy, which is the study of the human body, in regard to its framework. We take the body in pieces, as we would a watch, and find out all its parts and their uses. Secondly, Physiology, which teaches us the laws of life; or the knowledge of the play of the human machinery. This branch might be very rapidly taught, could we look through the healthy living body, and see all parts in motion, and understand that motion. Thirdly, Hygiene, as the French call it; or the study of the laws of relation. By this we mean, man's relation to air, water, and all the things or bodies around him, whether solid, liquid, or gaseous. Our health depends on our obedience to all the laws of these three great departments, especially the latter.

It is not pretended, of course, that such a knowledge of this great subject is needed by young men, as that which becomes a matter of necessity to the medical man, or the surgeon. *He* must not only have the same general knowledge which is needed by every young man, but a particular knowledge, so thorough as to be able to tell, when a finger is applied to any part of the surface of the body, what lies immediately under—what veins, blood-vessels, organs, &c.

When we announce the subject of Physiology, for a public lecture, not a few people think of it in the sense to which I have just referred, as it concerns the medical student. And, as a natural and almost necessary consequence, they revolt from it. "What time or means have we," they say, "for understanding this subject? Besides, what good would it do us? We are not to be doctors."

The same feeling exists, to some extent, when we talk of the necessity of having Physiology taught to children in schools—or, perchance, to Females. "What can possibly be the importance, to the young and to our wives, of this sort of knowledge?" they seem to say. "What would these innovators in Education have? Why, will they not ere long tell us our children must study farriery or ship-building?"

Others say, "Why! Physiology? What does that concern us, here in plain life—we who are obliged to earn our bread in the sweat of our face?" as if Physiology was something like star-gazing, or star-studying. Or, as if he who studied it must at least come to know under what planet he was born, and whether, in his temperament, he is ruled by Mars, Venus, or Mercury.

Others, again, who admit, in part, the utility

of this science, as it is taught by its most competent professors or teachers, seem to suppose it useful to them as a means of becoming their own doctors, or the doctors of others, when they are actually diseased. Of its importance, as a means of prevention, they have scarcely a single adequate idea.

When, however, they have read and approved of the little work called the "House I Live in," and are told they have been all this while reading Physiology, they seem to be surprised. "Why, if this is Physiology," they say, "there can be no objection to having every body study it. We should even like to study it more ourselves!" And now it becomes a matter of comparatively little difficulty to introduce it into our schools.

But I suppose that to several thousands of the young men who will read this letter, the introduction of Physiology into our schools will seem to come too late. They will, indeed, rejoice that their younger brothers and sisters are privileged so highly; and that the world, in general, is to be thus blessed But they will mourn over their own loss, and ask us how it can be in any measure restored.

What young men of the generation already risen have to do for themselves, in this matter, is to hear lectures in the first place. Not every thing that comes along ; but only such as have been most approved. These are of two kinds. 1st. Those which are illustrated by manikins. 2d. Those which teach the laws of health, without going so much into first principles.

Among the former are the lectures of Dr. Wieting, Dr. Darling, Dr. Cutter, and Mrs. Wright. Among the latter are those of Dr. Mussey, the Fowlers, Mrs. Gove, and myself.* Both these classes of lectures are important. The first class give you the outlines or elements ; the second go more into detail. Nevertheless, if you cannot find time to attend to them all, at least endeavor to hear the latter.

These lectures, duly attended to, will rouse you to the necessity of reading something on the same subject. You will find no periodical

* Mr. Graham's Lectures included both these departments —bnt he seems to have withdrawn from the field.

6*

exactly adapted to your wants—but many volumes of standard works—among which are those of the Combes, of Sweetser, of the Fowlers, of Graham, and a part of my own works. If you read but one, however, read Combe's Constitution of Man.

And if convinced, by lectures, reading and reflection, or in any other way, of the vast importance of obeying not only the great Creator's moral laws, but also his physical ones, there is one thing more for you to do, and that immediately. It is to act up to the knowledge you already possess. Do what your consciences testify to you is right. He that doeth truth—moral or physical—cometh to the light.

Really, my young friends, I know of no one subject, so rarely forced upon your notice, as the world now is, and yet so immensely important to your happiness as this same thing —this obedience to physical law—the laws of Anatomy, Physiology, and Hygiene. Be persuaded then, oh be persuaded, to make them, next to the laws contained in the Bible, the man of your counsel and the guide of your youthful steps.

In doing so, you will reap a rich reward in personal enjoyment. The value of each day of your life will be greatly increased; and your loss of time by ill health greatly diminished. You will begin, then, to know what was meant by the little scrawl of poetry, in the Library of Health, entitled "Morning all day." Your strength and vivacity and cheerfulness, like mine, will hold out every day, till the evening shades appear and beckon you to repose.

You will also add, under Providence, several years to your lives—Dr. Mussey is accustomed to say, so it has been reported—about twelve or fifteen. I suppose fewer than twelve, however. An average increase of five or six years to an individual, in the present generation, is all I should dare to hope, and almost as much as I dare to desire. Sudden and rapid changes are seldom durable.

But if no more than I have supposed can be done for the passing generation, much more can be done for the next, and for the third still more; and so on. If the work of reformation, on physical and physiological principles, can be once fairly begun and properly persevered in, I see no reason why life may not be lengthened, in the course of five or six centuries, to several hundred years, and the value of each year be doubled and tripled.

LETTER XV.

PHRENOLOGY.

THAT Phrenology, in its first or leading principles—that the brain is the material organ of the mind, that different mental faculties have connection with different parts of the brain, &c., &c.—is true, I can no more doubt than I could doubt the law of gravitation. But that every thing which is called Phrenology is worthy of your confidence, is quite another question.

After the study of Physiology, generally, I hope you will pay some attention to Phrenology. It is a branch of Physiology, but a most important branch. The material organ of the mind is not so large as some of the other organs of the body—systems, rather—

such as the machinery of locomotion or of digestion; still it has a very commanding influence. It is, to the confederate human system, what Massachusetts is to the confederated political system of our country. But of this I have spoken elsewhere.

Of course, I do not expect you to become adepts in this science. What you need, is a practical general knowledge of the subject, such as you may obtain from Combe's and Fowler's Phrenology, and from the various works, both periodical and otherwise, of these two individuals, especially the latter. There are two of these Fowlers, however; but I have been most acquainted with the works of the eldest, O. S. Fowler. I recommend to you, in particular, their Phrenological Journal. They have, it may be, their faults; but they certainly have many excellencies. What some call visionary in their works, more frequently deserves the name of soundly sensible. In truth few works in such a style, contain more "sound, *roundabout* common sense," than those of the Fowlers.

As I said of your study of general Physiology, so I must say, and with still more of emphasis, in regard to the study of Phrenology, make every thing practical. Apply the subject to your own personal improvement, either immediately or prospectively. What you need, is to be prepared for the great duties of life, which are so soon to devolve upon you, —some of which, indeed, always have, in a degree, borne upon you. There are duties to yourself—your friends—the world. There are duties to body, and duties to soul.

Set not out, in these studies, with too many prejudices. Hold yourselves every where open to conviction. And if convinced you have a deficiency in your mental, moral, or corporeal structure, seek to supply it in the best possible manner. Observe, that I do not say in the most *speedy* manner, for the most *rapid* cure, moral or physical, is seldom so good, in the end, as the slower one. Indeed, he who is ardent and resolute in the great work of self-education and improvement, should ever have for his motto: " Make haste slowly."

There is one fact, which, to my own apprehension, speaks loudly in favor of the study of Phrenology, and indeed of Physiology generally. I never met with a man who had read the best works, on these subjects, who was not much more happy and much more efficient in his employment or profession, than he would probably have been in his ignorance.

In traversing our country, I meet with a minister, here and there, who has investigated this great subject. The style of his preaching is much modified by it. His people will sometimes tell me that he has interested them more of late, than formerly; and they wonder what is the cause. Occasionally, I have been struck with the power of a preacher in the pulpit who was an entire stranger to me; and on inquiry have been not a little gratified to find that he had become a student of physical law, no less than of moral.

The other evening I heard an advocate of temperance speak. I had heard lectures on all departments of this subject before, and had lectured much myself. Judge, then, of my feelings, when I found near the close of the lecture, that he was not merely acquainted with the general laws of Physiology, but that

Phrenology was also a favorite study with him.

That I am liable to a little mistake on this point, either from prejudice or prepossession, is most certainly true. But then I do not believe I can be *wholly* mistaken. When a minister preaches in such a manner as to take a new hold upon me and every body else—when, in fact, he proclaims physical law, no less than moral and religious—I cannot but know it.

And when I find a young mechanic, or man ufacturer, or farmer, who, by the acknowledgment of all around him (most of whom know not the cause, and can, therefore, have no prejudice against him) has, of late, made great progress, especially, as a man of sound sense, and has come to tower a head and shoulders, like Saul, above his fellows; and then, on inquiry, I find he has been studying George Combe, or O. S. Fowler, or all of us and our associates in this department how can I be mistaken?

LETTER XVI.

PHYSIOGNOMY.

I HAVE had some experience in this matter of practical Physiognomy, which may possibly be of service to young men; and which I am quite willing they should avail themselves of. Perhaps, indeed, I set out, in life, with more tact at detecting men's character by their faces than some people. In any event, I early *possessed* this tact, whether it was acquired or natural.

Without having been a business man, in the common sense of the term, I have, for many years of my life, had a great deal to do with men of business in nearly every possible way. I have made it my rule to judge as well as I could concerning them, by their features and other externals; and if I thought them worthy of confidence, have taken and treated them as honest men till experience compelled me to do otherwise.

Now, in pursuing this course, I have generally succeeded in carrying forward my plans, though not in every instance, without embarrassment. Had I followed my own first convictions, I should seldom have suffered. In nearly every instance in which I have been a pecuniary loser—and these instances have been frequent—I have suffered from yielding to the opinions of others, instead of following my own judgment.

For example, I had bought a building lot, and wished to dig a cellar, and proceed to erect a house. While surveying the site, a stranger came to me—indeed the people of the neighborhood were all strangers to me—and wished to dig my cellar. I was not pleased with his appearance, and did not say much about employing him.

On inquiring, at the village near by, who were the best masons in that vicinity, I was at once referred to this very same man. Others were indeed named, but the former seemed to have the preference. I asked for specimens of his work; they were shown me, and were satisfactory. Of his honesty, I could learn nothing in particular, or of his general habits. It did not, however, appear that he was intemperate or openly vicious. In fine, I yielded to the judgment of others, and employed him.

This was the beginning of a series of difficulties that never terminated till I had not only suffered much, in various ways, especially by a total disregard of promise, but had even become involved in a serious lawsuit. Whereas, had I followed my convictions, concerning the indications of his physiognomy, I should have escaped.

It has been so in several other instances. The conclusion to which I have been driven is, to follow out my convictions of truth and duty in these cases for the remainder of my days—in other words, to yield to the claims of physiognomy. And if you have any tacı in ascertaining character by the face, I hope you will pursue the same course. It may save you as many thousands of dollars, as I have lost, besides much time and trouble and regret.

LETTER XVII.

TRAVELLING.

YOUNG men, with few exceptions, are fond of travelling; and in these days, the far greater part of them have more or fewer oportunities for gratifying their inclination. It is as rare now, to find a young man of thirty, who has not been beyond the limits of his native state, as it was thirty years ago, when I began to be a traveller, to find one who *had* been.

And yet it is of little consequence to travel, if we do not make a wise use of the privilege. If all a young man cares for, is to go from public house to public house, and eat at the most luxurious table, and sleep in the costliest apartments, he may almost as well remain within the range of the smoke of his own chimney.

Or if he loves to go abroad, chiefly to note the fashions, and watch the different exteriors of buildings, villages, and fields—to sneer at this, laugh at that, or fall into vexation with the other;—if this is his chief object, he might nearly as well be at home. He will certainly be more useful at home, if well employed there.

Or if, again, the most he cares for is to break life's monotony, "while away" the time, and as he is wont to say, enjoy life, when in reality he only means by enjoying life, laboriously doing nothing; in this case, too, travelling will be of very little service to him, as a means of making him either wiser or better. Nor will it mend the matter much, if he smoke double the number of cigars abroad that he does in the same time at home.*

* A ship-master in Barnstable county, Massachusetts, told me that in going, a few years since, to Gibraltar, he had a passage of thirty-one days, during which time he smoked 800 good Spanish cigars, besides chewing twenty-four ounces of tobacco. A bear, a marmot, or a bat, in a state of hyberna-

If temperance, and even abstemiousness are required of young men, in order that they may be profited, it is above all when they are travelling. I pity the young man who does not understand this, and sometimes wish I could point him as an example, to my more fortunate, and therefore more happy experience. Many have been farther from home, while few have travelled more than myself.

This remark may prepare the minds of my readers for the assertion, that it does not make so much difference as many young men suppose, *where* they travel, as the *use* they make of their opportunities. Some will learn more by travelling who do not go a thousand miles from home, than others who circumnavigate the globe.

I recommend to every young man, in the first place, to travel with his eyes open. I believe I have elsewhere said, that one great difference among men arises from the fact, that some of them see the world as they pass through it, while others blunder through it

tion, had it vocal organs, might as well talk of enjoying life, as men who thus stupefy themselves with tobacco.

with their eyes half shut. Much of our knowledge, as you know, comes to us through the medium of the senses, especially the eyes.

In the next place, what I would advise you to do while reading a book, I would advise you to do while travelling, viz.: have a memorandum or blank-book, with a pencil, and note down every passing occurrence that in any way interests you, and not only note the facts, but also your own reflections on them at the time.

If you are skilful at drawing, you will also find it useful to sketch many things which you observe—not merely a few elegant edifices, but curious trees, plants, flowers, implements of husbandry, mechanics or manufactures—or it may be, some curious bird or animal. Or if you are so unfortunate as not to have received any instruction in the art of drawing, still I would draw as well as possible, and persevere. There is much in the little word, TRY.

Do not travel merely to tell, when you get home, what you have seen, and heard, and known; although you are certainly bound to be influenced in some degree, by motives of this kind. An Apostle has said, "Forget not to do good, and communicate," and one means of doing good is to communicate, in one way or another, what we have learned.

Avoid reading while you are travelling. I do not presume, in this remark, that any whom I address, will read while they are travelling, for the sole purpose of making people believe they are very *learned*, or at least very *fond* of learning. And yet I have, in the course of my life, met with such persons. I knew one physician who used to read in his carriage, for the sole purpose, as I then thought—and so thought many others—of having the mass of those who saw him, believe he was a great student. And I have seen a few young persons of both sexes, who had a great many books around them, for the very same reason that they had a great deal of furniture in their rooms—not that it was needful, but to make a fine appearance.

In general, *walk* the country, if you can afford to do so. Never ride, if you can help it. I grant there are many difficulties in the way of walking; but then there are many advantages.

One is, that you will be at liberty to stop when and where you please, in order to note facts, or make your sketches or observations. But I have not time to enter upon the reasons very fully.

Should you need examples of the kind to encourage you, they are at hand. We need not speak of those ancient times, when almost every body walked, but may as well come near our own. Alfred the Great was a walker. So was the famous Count Fellenberg, of Hofwyl, in Switzerland. Wealthy as he was, he made the tour of Europe on foot, and this, too, of choice. I once planned to do so, but was prevented from carrying my plan into execution. Burritt, the learned blacksmith, travels much, as I understand, in the same way.

One or two cautions will be necessary before I conclude. Most travellers, in passing through a country, see only some of its larger features, so to call them. They see the high mountains, the large rivers, lakes, and cascades, the caves and hot-springs, and the larger cities and villages, but pass over the smaller things. Still more apt are they to forget to notice men, and above all, to study character. Remember that the study of the Christian temple—the human being—is of far more consequence to you, as a young man, than the study of St. Paul's, or St. Peter's, or Westminster Abbey.

Remember, too, wherever you go, the rights of your fellow-travellers, both as regards seats and a thousand other things. Some young men are so exceedingly selfish, that they will not rise up before the old—hardly before women and children. Nor is this all. If they have offensive personal habits, they are not at all careful to conceal them—partly, it may be, because they are among strangers. A young man will smoke in company, if he may, when among strangers, who would not venture to do so, *in similar circumstances, at home.*

Finally—for I must not enlarge—remember in travelling, more than almost any where else, the good old maxim, "Every one should mind his own business." Do not suppose the injunction clashes with one already given—to do good and communicate. What I now say has regard to your own personal safety and

happiness, more than any thing else. Some young men are always getting into difficulty when they travel, go where they may; while others never have much trouble any where. The latter you will find, on a close examination, mind their own business—the former do not. They can scarcely go from Boston to Cambridge, or from New-York to Brooklyn, without getting into difficulty, or, at least, without carrying bowie-knife or pistol.

I had the pleasure of an intimate acquaintance with the late Rev. Wm. C. Woodbridge, the Geographer. Few men of fifty years of age, have travelled more than he. Besides being familiar with nearly every part of the United States, he went for several successive winters to the West Indies, and made three or four voyages to Europe and the Mediterranean. In middle-Europe, or in various parts of Germany, and in Switzerland, he resided as many as six or eight years; perhaps eight or ten. In truth, he was as familiar with many of the countries and cities of both the Old and the New World, as most of us are with the town and county in whch we reside. And yet I have heard this same Mr. Woodbridge affirm, that he never, in all his life, carried with him any weapon of defence—not so much as a cane; and what is still more to the point, never had the slightest occasion to use any such weapon. While it is literally true, that a young relative of his at Cambridge, was unwilling to cross the bridge to Boston unarmed.

"Alcott," said an old schoolmaster and traveller, to me one day, thirty years ago, as I was about to set out on a long journey, "I have travelled in thirteen of the United States, and never yet had a quarrel with any man." "Can you tell me your secret," I said, "for preserving peace? "I have no secret about it," he replied, "except to mind my own business."

This lesson, as I trust, was not lost upon me. I have been a traveller in more than thirteen States, and have been familiar with almost every town, and village, and neighborhood in some of them, without having a quarrel, or the beginning of a quarrel with a single individual.

So it is, in no small degree, in regard to the *danger* of being molested in travelling.

I grant there are dangers to be encountered from accident and otherwise. I grant there are dangerous places. The worst, however, are those into which you are likely to be led by your appetites, lusts, or passions. As to the danger of being attacked, &c., I have found that they who take a prudent care of themselves, usually go safe through the world; while those who do not mind their own business, are the very persons who tell you about their hair-breadth dangers and escapes, and how necessary it is for you to arm yourself against those dangers.

LETTER XVIII.

CONSCIENTIOUSNESS.

It has been said that there is not much conscientiousness in the world. By this however is meant, as I suppose, that there is not much, in comparison of what there should be. For if, by conscientousness, or conscience, is meant a sense of right and wrong, there must be a degree of conscientiousness, one would think, in every human being who has passed the merest threshold of existence. But a trifling degree or amount, so to speak, of this quality, multiplied by the hundreds of millions that inhabit our earth at a given time, is an aggregate not to be despised. It supposes, or rather proves, a condition of things very different from what would be in a world which conscientiousness had not yet entered, or from which it had been entirely eradicated.

It is no part of my purpose to enter, here. upon the mooted discussion what conscience is. On the contrary, I take for granted, what I am sure nobody will dispute, that every one has this conscience; and proceed to such a course of remark, as I think the urgency of the case demands.

For that the case is an urgent one, no one at all acquainted with the facts, will for a moment presume to doubt. I admit—I have already done it—that there is an aggregate of conscientiousness in the world, that is by no means despisable. The Pagan has it, when he hangs on hooks fastened to his flesh, or throws himself under the car of the Juggernaut. The Mohammedan has it, when he pursues with fire and sword, those whom he wishes to convert to his faith. The Christian has it, when he conforms to a known law of a superior order.

I do not by any means affirm, that he who hangs on hooks fastened through his side, or compels his neighbor by fire or sword, to embrace his religion, acts up to the dignity of even *his* lower conscience. All I affirm is that he has his conscientiousness. But if this be so, what then do you mean, I shall be asked, when you complain of a want of conscientiousness in the world, and speak of the case as an urgent one? The want of which I complain is a comparative one. Our standard of right and wrong, in this enlightened age and country, is very high; and therefore, to whom much is given, of the same will much be required.

It is not a few religious duties, or a few important relations, merely, in regard to which we are to be conscientious. It is not on occasions, or set times, or particular seasons alone, but on all occasions, times and seasons. Whatever is worth doing is worth doing well, says an old and very true saying. And a higher authority than any other has enjoined upon us: "Whether ye eat or drink, or whatever ye do, do all to the glory of God."

But if whatever we do is to be done right—to the glory of God—then it should be done conscientiously. And we have no more right to set aside conscience in one case than in another. Not that all laws, moral, religious, and secular, are of equal authority, so as to make the voice of conscience equally loud. Still her decisions concerning the smallest matters, when they have been made—and made they should continually be—are as truly binding as those which relate to matters of the first magnitude.

A young man in Boston—a teacher—with whom I had the pleasure of a long and valuable acquaintance, was one day conversing on the subject to which I have now called your attention, when he suddenly observed: "Why, my dear sir, there is a large range of human action that has no right or wrong about it."

I have seldom been more struck with surprise, in my whole life, than with this singular answer, especially as coming from an intelligent and good man. Had he read Paul? I thought. And accordingly, I asked him if he had not. "Oh, yes," he said; "but this saying of Paul, in this particular, must be understood with some limitation. He *cannot* mean that there is a right and wrong to every small concern of human life. The matter of gratifying the appetite must be one of these. Why, we are creatures of instinct, in many things; and our actions are matters of instinct, with which right and wrong have nothing to do."

It is hardly necessary for me to say to you that this reasoning was at war with facts—the Bible itself being competent testimony. And yet it is—practically so, at least—the reasoning of thousands. But men ought to know better than to have doubts on such a subject about which the Bible is so explicit.

I must maintain, moreover, that it is according to right reason to suppose that we should be conscientious in these matters. Why, there must be right and wrong and conscience somewhere, all admit—but where? Is it in regard to larger matters alone? Why, these but seldom recur, whereas the smaller matters of life are of almost perpetual recurrence.

Or if it should be still urged that there are certain small matters, which are so very small that they have no moral character to them, will any one point out the precise line or degree at which they commence? In the descending scale, for example, which is the last of the series of matters so large as to have character to it, and which the first so trifling as to have no character?

For until some one will do this, I shall deem it my duty to maintain that there neither *is* nor *can be* any dividing line. And as there would be a very great difference, some placing the line at one point of elevation, some at another, I shall not hold myself obliged to pay much attention to any dividing line, till one is mentioned in which all or nearly all agree. But this is not, in the nature of things, likely to happen.

I do not suppose mankind deem it their duty to be conscientious for more than one-eighth or one-tenth of their time. Of course, the hours for sleep are not included in that tenth. But there is only one day in seven, during any considerable part of which, the mass of mankind give much heed to the voice of conscience. Even on this day, the far greater number have no conscience in regard to any thing more than a few stated hours. The rest they consider themselves as allowed to eat, drink, or sleep away, as they may choose.

And as for the six week days, the heavenly monitor seems to have nothing to do on these, except to prompt us on a few occasions as at morning and evening devotions—at stated meals—and in times of sickness, adversity, or dissolution. Or if he comes in the still small voice, we silence it amid the din of business or the hurry of amusement.

Strange that it should be so. Well might a venerable ancient, who was looking over the volume of inspiration, and thinking of its demands, cry out, Blessed Lord, either these are not thy words, or we are not Christians! Blessed Lord, I will add, in relation to our present subject, either the volume of Truth is not thine, and reason is not thine, and we are not thy children, or else we fall far short—I might almost say infinitely short of the standard of conscientiousness, thou hast thyself established. Send down upon us then, thy heavenly wisdom, that we may amend our lives, and spend the remainder of them according to thy most reasonable and most divine will and word.

LETTER XIX.

LOVE OF EXCITEMENT.

FEW topics could be selected of greater importance to the young, than that which is intended by the caption of this article. And if I should fail to make it appear so, let the blame fall on me—rather on my manner of handling the subject—and not on the subject itself which I have chosen.

When I speak of the evils of excitement, however, I usually mean an undue or excessive love of it. To avoid excitement wholly, would be to go out of the world—and perhaps out of the universe. Air and water, in a sense, are excitants, although it is true that without them we could not survive a moment. But there is a wide difference between excitement and over-excitement—or in other words, between a reasonable use of excitement, and excess in its use—induced by an undue fondness or love of it. Stimulus, stimulus! excitement, excitement! this is the universal cry.

This is an evil which prevails every where, and in almost every form. Nay, more; this undue fondness for excitement of body or mind, is not only every where prevalent, but every where increasing; and threatens, unheeded and unopposed, the ruin of the whole rising generation. Against it, therefore, I feel compelled to lift up a warning voice. Let him hear who hath ears.

Some there are who meet us at the threshold, by what they suppose to be an insurmountable difficulty, and gravely tell us that no line can be drawn between that amount, or degree, or kind of stimulus which is healthful, and that which is unhealthful or injurious. But this is a mistake. Excitants or stimuli, cease to be healthful or salutary in their effects, precisely when and where they cease to invigorate body or mind, and when their effects begin to prove debilitating.

What, it will be asked, is the rule, then? Is it to make one's own experience his guide? I answer, yes; as far as our own experience goes. This, however—the experience of any one individual, I mean—will go but a little way. Much will remain—very much—to be determined by the experience of others, and especially by those forms of experience which are embodied into science.

To make plain my meaning, take the case of alcoholic drinks. Now, there is a use of these drinks, whose consequences in their direct effects on himself, no young man could mistake. The greatest ignoramus I have ever seen intoxicated, knew he had been too far—had indulged his love of excitement to excess—when fairly recovered to his former condition. The prodigal in the gospel understood perfectly well where he had been, when he "came to himself." And yet there are other uses of alcoholic drink, which, judging *merely* from one's own experience, produce no evil effects, but concerning which, science has told us, within a few years, a very different story.

Experience on a large scale, embodied into

science—the sciences of chemistry, physiology, &c.—has told us that alcohol in every form and in every degree, when introduced into the healthy, living, human system, is a foe, and a foe continually, until it is expelled. And more than this has it told us—that its effects are permanent, and even transmissible to other and unborn generations. That though the use of a moderate quantity of wine, cider, beer, or diluted spirits, gives warmth and strength, and activity at the time, yet it weakens body and mind both, in the end.

I do not deny that one's own experience, *enlightened by the study of the sciences*, would go very far towards enabling us to judge correctly on this subject. Indeed, this is what has just now been affirmed. As a student of chemistry and physiology, I know well, while under the influence of half a gill of toddy, a gill of wine, or a tumbler of beer or ale, that I have gone too far. I know it by a debility of the heart and arteries.

For what if these beat a little faster than usual? This does not indicate an increase, but a diminution of strength and vigor. The pulse in a fever, though more frequent than before, is not the stronger, but the weaker for it. And when we drink alcohol, in any shape whatever, the arterial action is quickened by it.

And here, by the way, I lay down one general rule, by means of which most persons may know when they have, and when they have not, passed the line of healthy excitement. I will not say that the rule admits of no exceptions, for like most general rules, it may admit a few. The rule is this. As that which strengthens does not increase the activity of the heart and arteries, but on the contrary causes them to beat more full and strong, so that which weakens or debilitates, *does* increase this activity, and should therefore be avoided.

Or if there seem one glaring exception to this rule, staring us full in the face—I allude to the effects of exercise—the rule may be modified a little. Whatever so increases the activity and strength of the pulse, as to be followed by a debility which, when the system is restored to its balance is not fully removed, must be hurtful.

Need I say here, that all alcoholic drinks—down to the weakest home-brewed beer, if it has fermented at all—are of this description? That tobacco is another; opium another; coffee another; tea another, &c? Every sensible young man who has used any of these, knows that they exhilarate him; yet he knows, too, that after having used them once, if he do not repeat his dose, he is ere long debilitated as the *consequence* of their use.

There is one law which deserves to be better known to the young than it sometimes is. The smaller the amount of alcohol or stimulus which is taken into the system—provided it is enough to be at all appreciable—the greater the derangement, if not the debility which follows, in *proportion* to its quantity.

Understand me, however, my young friends. I do not mean to say, or to intimate, that half a gill of small beer, or weak wine, will injure you, as much as the same quantity of full proof rum, gin, or brandy; but only much more in proportion to *the quantity of alcohol* it contains.

To some, I am well aware, there will be nothing new in this last statement. To a few, however, the doctrine will be strange; and they will be disposed to ask, "How can these things be? How is it possible that a smaller dose of poison—for poison we take it to be—can affect the living system more injuriously, in proportion to its quantity, than a large one? Are beer, cider, wine, coffee and tea, more injurious, then, in proportion to the amount of poisonous or medicinal substance they contain, than rum, gin and brandy?" I answer, that they are so.

Do you wish for reasons? First, it must be so, from the nature of the case. The larger the quantity of poison we take, provided we do not take enough to overwhelm the powers of life at once, the greater the probability that there will be a reaction, and that the offending substance will be thrown out of the system, either upward or downward. Whereas in the case of the very small quantity, the system is not so much disturbed; and the little which is tkaen steals its march, as it were, upon the system; and becoming incorporated into it, has its full pernicious effect.

Secondly, we establish this doctrine—which you are pleased to call a new or strange one—by analogy. If we wish to produce a merely local impression on the system, by some strong medicine—say calomel—we throw a pretty large dose, perhaps twelve or twenty grains, into the stomach. A reaction soon follows, and it is thrown off.

But if, on the contrary, our aim is to produce a general impression—in other words, if we wish to poison or salivate with it—we give half a grain, or a quarter of a grain. And the repetition, for a few times only, of these minuter doses, will bring about the result we desire. It is so with alcohol among the rest. For, what is alcohol but a medicine, wherever we find it?

I might add a third species of proof on this point, were further proof needful. They who use alcohol in large measure, once in a month, or once in two months, and then use nothing but water the rest of the time, though they may, and doubtless do, injure themselves to the full extent which has ever, by any finite being, been supposed, do not, after all, impair their health or diminish their longevity so much as those who sip a little every day, and yet are never disguised by it. Nor are the ill effects on the offspring of the former, so obvious as they are on those of the latter.

Indeed one remark might be applied to all medicinal substances, from alcohol, opium, calomel and tobacco, down to beer, coffee, tea, pepper, saleratus, vinegar, &c. The strength they give is not by adding nutriment to the system, but by exciting the nerves and brain. They give strength, I admit, but it is only by tickling the nerves, as it were, and hence the strength is temporary, and leaves the system more debilitated than it found it. It also increases the temptation to repeat the dose.

I wish young men could fully understand and appreciate the views I have here faintly and imperfectly, but yet in all sincerity and honesty set forth. I wish they could fully know that all the extra warmth and strength they obtain, by drawing out nervous energy any faster than it is naturally drawn out by those articles of food and drink which are properly converted into blood, to nourish the body, are at the future expense of that nervous system and the other machinery which furnish it.

For, suppose that correct views on this subject were to cut off every conscientious young man from the use, not only of all exciting—i. e., over-exciting—drinks, but also from all kinds of medicine,* however small or trifling, would they not be gainers by it in the end? Admit that it should be found out, gradually, that many of what are called condiments or seasonings, were also medicinal substances; and that they were, each in its turn, abandoned—what then? Who wishes to gratify his natural fondness for excitement, at the expense an impaired constitution for himself and his

* This remark is not intended to apply to the case of those who have submitted themselves to the general direction of the physician. They, of course, have no safe way but to take whatever he orders for them. Even if he orders poison they should take it—and this, too, whether in large or small quantities.

posterity? Who does not, on the contrary, wish to do right and reap the consequences?

But I might go entirely beyond the region of selfishness, and appeal to your sense of duty to God and man—to God, I mean, and the human race. Have you a right to gratify yourself—your nervous sensibilities, I mean—at the expense of your health, or at the hazard of impairing the constitutions of those who may come after you?

LETTER XX.

ON PURITY

"He is a very *pure* young man," said a friend to me, many years ago, concerning a young schoolmaster to whom I had just been introduced, in eastern Connecticut. A very pure young man! I said to myself. What sort of a recommendation is this?—for as a recommendation it was certainly intended.

It is not necessary, however, to live in this world half a century, in order to learn that purity is one of the highest possible recommendations, in either sex. We may learn it in half that time. I am always glad to find a young man or a young woman temperate, conscientious and industrious. But to find one who is pure, is still more than all this; for purity like charity covers a multitude of other transgressions.

You need not regard my opinion, on this subject, as standing alone. Paley, in his Natural Theology, represents purity of character as the hinge on which all else turns. And Paul, in his writings, especially in his letters to Timothy, repeatedly dwells on its importance. And as if to sum up every thing in one, he says to the latter on a certain occasion, very emphatically, "Keep thyself pure."

Indeed who that has studied the history of mankind, as it is in this particular, is at all surprised to find the great apostle of the Gentile world levelling some of his deadliest blows as a Christian warrior in this very direction? Who is not shocked at the very detail of the gross impurities he is obliged, in the very opening of his letter to the Romans, to charge on that then comparatively enlightened and elevated nation?

But if Rome—learned and polite Rome—was so bad, how was it with the rest of the nations around her? One may be guided by something more than conjecture, in this matter. The dark catalogue of vices which Paul charges upon the inhabitants of Asia Minor and Southern Europe is almost always headed by one or two—sometimes three or four—kinds of impurity. For example; adultery, fornication, uncleanness, and lasciviousness, stand in the foregound of the picture of Galatian vices; fornication and uncleanness in that of the Ephesians; fornication, uncleanness, inordinate affection, and evil concupiscence, in that of the Colossians; fornication and concupiscence in that of the Thessalonians; and fornication in that of the Corinthians.

The consequences of these evils are fearful, even in this world. They are not all, however, equally so. As it is in regard to other vices that each, if persisted in, has its appropriate disease, (drunkenness, for example, its delirium tremens,) so it is with all these. But I need not particularize. All diseases are, so far as I can learn, the penalties of transgression; but the penalty falls on some more, on others less directly. There are few that seem so much like the direct judgments of offended Heaven as that which falls upon gross impurity.

Short of this, however, there is much suffer ing, not only of the individual, but, as in the former case, of posterity also. The sins of parents, at least in their consequences, are visited upon children unto the third and fourth generation—probably to the twentieth. Scrofula, eruptions, gout, and I hardly know how many more diseases, are the frequent punishment of vice, as committed somewhere. A modern physiologist tells us that two-thirds of the diseases to which our race is liable, have their origin in the abuses to which I now refer.

Few are probably aware—medical men and physiologists excepted—to what an extent the least infringement of the Divine law, in these particulars, militates againt the well-being of our race. That the grosser forms of impurity are injurious—at least to others!—some will be ready to admit; though even here not a few are skeptical. But that licentiousness in every degree—from the more gross outbreakings, down to the mere thoughts and imaginations of the heart—more or less injures the health of all who indulge in it, is not, I believe, generally known; and is not usually believed when it is proclaimed.

Yet if there be a truth in the wide moral world, it is that every licentious action, word and thought—every one, I mean, which is truly of the licentious kind—as certainly injures the physical frame of him who indulges it, at least in some small degree, as the fountain, rivulet, and river lead to the mighty ocean!

But this is not all, nor the worst. The Scriptures of the Old and New Testament represent the human being—the body of course included—as the temple of the Holy Spirit; and while they accompany their exhortations to purity with proffers of the richest rewards, they also threaten, with the most fearful penalty, every profanation of that temple. Shall we experience the dreadful penalties annexed to impurity in this life, when we know, full well, that those penalties, dreadful as they may be to the sufferer, are but a prelude to suffering still greater, in that world of woe to which we are rapidly hastening?

That he has no trifling task to perform who would keep himself pure, is cheerfully admitted; nevertheless he cannot fail of having a full reward for his exertion even in this world. The consciousness of having in us a spirit of purity, is a powerful stimulus to every kind of activity. Whereas, the consciousness of impurity, makes us feel *meanly;* and unfits us, in a good degree, for the discharge of every duty.

"Blessed *are* the pure in heart," said our Saviour, and nothing could have been more timely or true. He did not say, Blessed *will be* the pure in heart. The blessing is immediate and future both. Purity has the promise, like godliness, both of this life, and that which is to come.

The sources of licentiousness in a world like our own, are almost endless. The mighty Mississippi does not burst forth a Mississippi at once. It is fed by the fountains and streams of a million of square miles. So with vice, especially that which we are now considering.

Let me notice, briefly, some of the sources of impurity which are most obvious and frequent, and against which, therefore, you will do well to guard; and not only to guard yourselves, but if it be more needful, your neighbors.

One is too much HEAT. This may be applied either *externally* or *internally*. *Externally*, as by too high a temperature in our rooms, too much clothing by night or by day, and atmospheric excitement acting upon the skin. But these last act also on the lungs, and therefore lead us to the consideration of *internal* sources of extra heat. These are an exciting or medicated atmosphere, exciting food and drink, useless medicine, exciting mental food, and excited feelings.

Against all these, and perhaps many others, every young man will do well to be on his guard, and that continually. Some of them are, of course, worse than others; but all are quite bad enough. No one of them can be long in operation, with safety; but the influence of two or three of them combined is, of course, much worse than that of any one acting singly. In general, let your motto be, Keep cool, keep cool.

Another source of impurity is UNDUE MENTAL EXCITEMENT. One effect of excessive mental excitement may be to produce internal heat upon the brain. Those who excite their brains too much, are often such as sit a good deal; which doubtless increases the determination of blood to the head; and is accompanied with the development of an unusual amount of heat. But apart from the ill effects of the heat, there seems to be a *reflex action*, whenever we drive the brain too fast, which has a direct tendency to excite impure thoughts and feelings, and, in various ways, to do much mischief.

For reasons, however, upon which I have not now room or disposition to enter, it would appear that the perusal of works of imagination and fiction, have a more obvious, certain, and immediate tendency to licentious feelings, than works of a graver sort, and the pursuit of mathematics, and other grave studies.

Another fruitful source of the evil in question, is indulgence itself. As face, in the glass, answers to face, and as like, by a general, if not inevitable law of Nature's God, produces its like, so every degree and form of impurity, in thought, word, and deed, tends to increase the maddening flame, and endanger our destruction.

Young men do not seem to understand this. Not a few of them seem to suppose, that just as the newly formed gas in the fermenting cask will sometimes, for want of vent, burst forth with such violence as to destroy the cask, and scatter abroad its contents, so if there be no such thing as giving vent to the appetites, the system must suffer. They suppose, in one word, there must be an explosion; and that this explosion, like those of Etna and Vesuvius, serves the system an important purpose.

Such young men ought, however, to know that, before the age of twenty-five, if not afterward, every improper action, word, and thought, is like seed cast into a luxuriant soil, and brings forth a new crop of the same kind. The greater the indulgence, the louder the cry of the system for its repetition. It is, in this respect, like the horse leech's daughter mentioned by Solomon, that cried incessantly, Give, give.

I have said "before the age of twenty-five," because prior to this period, no young man has any thing to do—in virtue of the laws of physiology—with any of the forms of indulgence to which I refer, unless he is willing to inflict an injury on his whole system, physical and mental, from which he can never fully recover. Indulgence, after this period, is fruitful enough of evil consequences, but it is much more so before it.

At present I will only add, that one common and prolific source of improper and impure feelings is bad associates—whether of one sex or the other. These are very common, and very influential. Who does not know that example is almost omnipotent? Yet that same example is as powerful for evil as for good—perhaps more powerful. It is so, if the general tendencies of human nature are downward, rather than upward. It is so, if the public opinion concerning men, in all ages, has been true. It is so, if the testimony of Revelation, corroborating that of reason and public opinion, has any weight. It is so, if the promises of God have any thing to invite us, or his threatenings any thing to excite our terror.

LETTER XXI.

MODELS AND MODEL CHARACTER.

In my letter on politics, I shall urge upon you the study of the history and geography of our country, as the basis of that subject. Closely connected with these, however, is the study of *biography*. I wish this last were made a fundamental branch in every public or common school. For to say nothing, now, of the historical and political information which, when properly written, it communicates, it is still more valuable, in another respect, to which I would respectfully call your attention.

Young men, to an extent greater or less, are chameleon-like. They take a tinge, so to speak, from the company they keep; especially if it is *much* kept. Nay, they are often affected for life by the society of an individual for merely half an hour. It is so as regards coming in contact with character through the medium of books.

Now, biography enables us to associate (to all practical interests and purposes) with men of all ages and all climes—with Moses, Joseph, David, Solomon, Isaiah, Homer, Confucius, Plato, Zeno, Paul, John, Franklin, Cuvier, and Howard. In the language of another, we are enabled, in this way, to "shake hands across oceans and centuries." And young men are often influenced almost as much by the men of other climes and ages with whom they thus shake hands, as by those whose hands they shake, from day to day, at home.

I knew a young man who was fond, to excess, of the writings of Franklin. Not only his philosophy, but his manners, habits, and style of writing charmed him, and at once became his model. The attachment to the Doctor led, in a practical point of view, to an intimate acquaintance. His efforts to imitate him were attended with great success. He became a "doer of good;" and learned, with

Franklin, to value highest, this species of reputation.

Others have taken, as their model, such men as Addison, Washington, or Byron. The result has been, in not a few instances, that they have approximated to the character they have labored to imitate. And Franklin, himself, in point of style, was a successful imitator of Addison.

No young man can know how much he is indebted to this species of influence. If the notion of Dr. Rush, that we are apt to resemble those by whose names we are called, especially when they have been greatly distinguished, is well founded, may it not be accounted for from the fact, that we are led, by the name, to become familiar with the biography of him who bore it; and thus in a degree to take him as a model?

Let me exhort every young man to select his model, and do it early in life. The earlier the better. I do not, indeed, mean to insist upon your copying any one character, exclusively; nor in fact upon your attempting a perfect copy of any body. Men are but fragments of men, after all; and do not deserve—the best of them—to be copied entire. Even the venerable Dr. Franklin himself is not an exception to the truth of this remark.

Perhaps it might be preferable to have before the mind's eye, as models, several different individuals. One may be our model in point of style, another in manners, another in philosophy, &c. On this last point, however, I speak with some diffidence, for want of sufficient experience.

Of one thing, however, I am certain; which is, that many excellent young men—I mean excellent in point of intention—accomplish but little in this world, because they attempt but little. The greater part, in truth, come into the world and pass through it as if they were without any definite aim and object. And as certainly as the stream never rises higher than the fountain whence it has its source, just so certainly will young men who aim at nothing, accomplish nothing.

I do not forget how apt I am to dwell on this topic—the low and unworthy aims of a great many young men. When you have had the experience of half a century, however, you will know how to excuse me. You will not only know how to excuse importunity and repetition, but also warmth.

A patient of mine, in one instance, who was dragging on an aimless existence, was told how to set his mark high, and was actually set to work. The result was, in a little while, very great improvement in his whole condition.

But I am inclined to digression. I have said that men are mere fragments of men—and that it is difficult, therefore, to find in any individual, a perfect model. There is one exception to the truth of this remark. In the man of Nazareth, we find a perfect model character. Happy the individual, young or old, who is wise enough to select his model in this divine direction.

Let no young man sneer at the idea of fixing on Jesus Christ as his model. Let him not say that men and manners in 1849, and in America, differ so greatly from the men and manners of Palestine in the days of our Saviour, that such a model is no model at all;

for it is not so. No man shall go before me in estimating the value of a Saviour for the "atonement's sake;" and yet no man shall go before me in valuing him as our exemplar. The Saviour was a model for the child, the youth, and the young man, no less than for the man of thirty.

True it is, we do not know that he was ever tried in all the circumstances of every young man's life; but only in all the essential points which are necessary to develope character. And as it seems to me, no young man can carefully study his character in all the points to which I refer, without understanding what is required in order to follow him.

Let Jesus Christ, then, my young friends, be your model man. Study, above all the rest, his biography. Find out, as soon as possible, what it is to act as he acted; and what he would do, governed by the great principles by which it is clearly seen he was governed, in all your circumstances. Find it out, I say, but do more. Yield yourselves up to be led by him. Were young men to do this, but for a single century, the world would again flourish as did Eden—nay, it would become as the garden of God.

If you call this preaching, be it so. How shall young men, any more than old men, "hear without a preacher?" You are fond of philosophy, I suppose—common sense philosophy. Now philosophy has had much to say, during the last century, about the influence of example. But who has not conceded that our Saviour's example may safely be imitated? Be philosophers, for once, and let the brightest example the world has yet seen, be more powerful with you than even his divine precepts.

LETTER XXII.

DECISION AND FIRMNESS.

The eminent John Foster has written a long essay upon the importance of Decision; and this essay of his has contributed more, perhaps, than all things else which he has written, to bring him into favorable notice. Indeed, had he written nothing else, this alone would have "immortalized" his name.

"Decision of character," says Mudie, on the observation of nature, "consists in the readiness and rapidity with which we can not only judge, but judge rightly. When genuine," he adds, "and exercised within the proper bounds, it is probably the most valuable temperament of mind that man can possess." No wonder, then, if in a series of letters to young men, I call attention to it, for a few moments.

It stands opposed, we are told, to that indecision which disqualifies a man for weighing evidence, and that fastidiousness in which time and attention are wasted upon trifles which form no important part of the evidence at all.

"Napoleon Bonaparte is perhaps," adds Mudie, "the most remarkable instance of decision of character, that occurs in well authenticated history;" and I have no doubt he was so. And yet, as the same excellent writer well observes, his history affords the most remarkable instance on record of the failure of that decision.

Ledyard, the American traveller, is usually set down as more remarkable than most men for decision of character. Perhaps Washington has as few superiors in this respect as any American, except Ledyard and President Jackson. And even these last were tempered a little too much with the excess of that other quality which I have taken for my motto, but which it is extremely difficult to blend with any thing else in just proportion.

"A genuine decided character—one which

will enable a man to carry all his plans into effect with success, and to ride buoyant upon every wave of the sea of trouble—is perhaps not to be obtained, at least early in life, without a certain degree of stubbornness; and as that stubbornness produces a sort of contempt for advice and new information, even in the case in which their aid would be most desirable, there is some danger of failure and reverse after success has lulled caution, and time begun to blunt the edge of observation.

"The man of truly decided character, must be one who is capable of taking long and clear views into the future; but as the past is the only telescope through which the future can be seen, the man of truly decided character must be an incessant, and also a silent observer from his youth."

To me it seems that little can be accomplished in this world, without decision and firmness both. And yet the great desideratum, during the whole work of self-education, consists in so tempering these together, that they may both accomplish their purposes without the excesses which have sometimes been charged against them, and to which it cannot well be denied they are liable.

If this book, and about a hundred others, from the same author, have been of any value to the world, it is owing, in no small degree, to a certain turn of life which might be named, and that turn was the result of decision of character

LETTER XXIII.

SETTING UP IN BUSINESS.

Since the Young Man's Guide was first written, one or two eminent men have most earnestly requested me to review the ground of an opinion expressed in that work, viz.: that young men are apt to assume the full responsibilities of business too early. I have done so; still, however, I am driven to the same conclusion as before.

The notion is prevalent among young men —it always has been so—that each new generation, especially their own, is wiser than that which preceded it. So that though most of you are well aware that your ancestors began business later than you, yet you seem to see in this, no reason why you should wait till you reach the same more advanced age. You honestly believe, no doubt, that you are as capable of succeeding at twenty or twenty-two, as they were at twenty-five or twenty-eight.

In most of the cities of the United States, young men set up for themselves in business by the time they are twenty-one; and not a few even earlier. And a majority of those now engaged in business—the active part of business I mean—are between twenty and thirty-five; perhaps I might even say between twenty and thirty. It is so in particular in New-York.

Now it was not always so. Men set up in business much earlier than formerly. Formerly, too, success was more certain than now. There were failures then, I well know; but they were not so frequent or so common. It could not be said then, as it now is, that ninety-five in a hundred of all our mercantile men fail once at least in their business lifetime, or that there are few men who succeed in business who have not made at least one failure.

Now who shall say that a state of things where failure in business is almost universal; and success, without a failure, only an exception to the general rule, is not owing, in a very large degree, to the fact that the young rush into business too early? Yet since so many *do* say this, let us review the grounds of such an opinion. Let us see who, in this particular, are the wisest, we or our fathers.

Professional men, beyond a doubt, often fail of success because they assume the responsibilities of their profession too early. Even if they set out with sound constitutions, they very often destroy themselves by the age of thirty-five; or at least render themselves useless if not burdensome. But when they often set out, as is a matter of fact, with scrofulous or consumptive constitutions, this increases the evil, both as regards tendencies and results.

These remarks are particularly applicable to young clergymen, but will serve for the latitude and longitude of young men of other professions. The physician, as a general fact, sets up for himself a little later, and perhaps also the lawyer. But the teacher breaks down almost as early as the clergyman; and for nearly the very same reasons. I have known but one teacher who lasted to be useful in his profession fifty years; and he began his studies late—I believe at about twenty-five years of age.

Pres. Humphrey, late of Amherst College, appears to be of opinion that young men ought not to assume the full responsibilities of preacher and pastor till about thirty years of age. Other wise men entertain a similar opinion. And you know the Jewish rule—a rule to which it would seem our Saviour chose to conform. He did not enter upon the full responsibilities of his mission till he was over twenty-nine—that is till he "began to be about thirty."

I am not disposed to attach too much importance to this particular period; but no man is a *man*, in the full sense of the term, till he is well nigh thirty. The bony frame is not fully consolidated till about twenty-five; and in some cases not till twenty-seven or twenty-eight. Then again the mental framework, so to call it, is of still slower growth. And once more;

the scrofulous are still longer in coming to maturity, or at least in becoming able to bear an average share of earth's responsibilities, than most other people.

Those who fall into mercantile pursuits—and of the readers of these remarks, not a few are supposed to be of this description—are little wiser in their course than those who betake themselves to the learned professions. They set out almost as unfavorably, rush forward as eagerly, and break down as early. Bright as their morning is—for scrofula is remarkable for the brightness it imparts—their sun sets ere they are aware, often before noon.

How have I been pained a thousand times, to see these buds of promise so early perish! The remark on infancy,—" Too bright to live long," and that on youth and adolescence,—" Death delights in a shining mark," mean something. They point to scrofula, " almost as sure as plummets fall." This prematurity —precocity rather—in body and mind, that delight us so much, are of ill portent. Give me the slower growth, and duller mental powers, in preference. I want no precocity—

no prematurity—no prodigies. I want no plants—human ones, at least—for hot-houses.

Young I—— was son of a clergyman of eminence, some twenty miles or more from Boston. He was a bud of promise, and unhappily was thought fit for the city counting-room, when his constitution required the air and exercise of his father's little farm. At sixteen he was a clerk in Washington-street. Scarcely out of his teens, his ambition was gratified with the full responsibilities of business. And what he could not do, towards destroying himself, during the six days, he made up, on the seventh, with Sabbath school. He died suddenly, and was buried with all the honors which are usually awarded, in these cases, by the ignorant and unthinking. Mysterious, it was said, by good men even, are the ways of Providence; and this, with a sigh, was all; except that they went on their way to train their sons to run the same race.

I will not deny—for I cannot conscientiously do so—that not a few of these precocious young men, will "make more money," were making money the great end and aim of life, by ten years of active effort between twenty and thirty, than by any ten years after that period. But grant even that a young man may "make his fortune" in that time, and then lay aside business, and live on his hastened earnings, still it does not follow that he has taken the wiser course.

If there were any method of ascertaining the exact yearly loss to society in consequence of acute disease—rendered severe and fatal by over-exertion of body and mind, amid a multiplicity of cares, many of which belong not at all to such early years—we should probably be astonished at the fearful aggregate.

Should it fall as low as thousands—I fear rather that it would rise to tens of thousands—the results would startle us. Place the number at 10,000, the average age at death at twenty-five; the average duration of human life at forty-five, and the value of time at only $250 a year; and yet we have an annual loss, in this respect, of $50,000,000. Will any of you say this is an over-estimate? I wish it might prove so.

But leaving this class, there is another which is little less to be pitied—I mean dyspeptics. Fewer young men become dyspeptics who engage in mercantile pursuits—I mean fewer in proportion to the whole number concerned —than of those who engage in sedentary occupations, such as shoemaking, tailoring, &c. And yet there are many merchants, and merchants' clerks, who suffer in this way. I suppose about 5000 of these last become dyspeptics every year.

These lose, (saying nothing of the bodily suffering, which some think worse than death,) at least half their time, for a period as long as the former. Here is an aggregate of $25,000,000.

But I have not yet done. We lose every year about 60,000 young people from consumption and scrofula. They are *almost always* precocious, and have been hurried into active life too soon. I suppose I am quite safe in placing the number of young men whose dissolution by consumption is hastened in this way, at 20,000 a year. Indeed, I am afraid this is much too low.

These die at an average age of thirty. They therefore lose fifteen years each ; besides an average of two years from sickness. Here is an aggregate of $95,000,000. Put together the three smaller aggregates I have made out, and we have a grand total of $170,000,000. Remember, moreover, that this loss is to be repeated, in the usual course of things, every year!

Now I ask the friends of going early into business, whether they really believe that society gains enough by it to compensate itself for all this loss. It will require a good many purchases and sales to clear $170,000,000 a year, or more than $5,000,000,000 every thirty years!

I have not taken into the account the medicine, and a thousand other things which I might have reckoned, because I would not seem to be extravagant. I will just add, however, that the value of the medical services and medicine these persons consume yearly, must rise above one million of dollars—while the loss of time to attendants and friends cannot be less than several millions.

They who complain of the doctrines of the "Young Man's Guide," should know what is the end—the dreadful end—of this rushing so early into business. They should know how many fail in business, as the consequence, and how many in health. They should make wise comparisons between those who serve a long apprenticeship to their employment—whether learned, mercàntile, mechanical or manufacturing—and those who do not.

And this it is—precisely this very thing—this apprenticeship—that I am about to recommend to you, my young friends. I know you are apt to revolt from it; but depend upon it, mere feeling, in this as well as in other matters, is blind. The intellect is the helmsman, and blind feeling must yield to her the pre-eminence.

I do not say you must serve, in every instance, seven, or ten, or twelve years. Circumstances may require a longer period in one case than in another. But be you sure of one thing—the longer you can serve in this way, provided you are *this side of thirty*, and are conscious you are every day growing wiser healthier and holier, the better for all your prospects will it be, whether near or remote.

Even if your highest aim were to make money, what I have said is worthy of your entire confidence. I have been young, and now am old, yet never have I seen the young man a loser even in a pecuniary point of view, from serving many long years as an apprentice or a journeyman.

Grant, as we have already done, that youth is more active—and that a young man will do more between twenty and forty, than between thirty and fifty; yet if, on the one hand, he is dead or as good as dead at forty, and on the other, able to go through with a second twenty years of hard labor, is he the loser? And this comparison has facts for its basis. It is far from being an exaggeration.

Perhaps I need not recur to my own experience in proof of the correctness of the views I present; but you must allow me to say, in this place, that so far as the experience of a single individual can go towards establishing a point of this kind, mine is in favor of a long *journeymanship*. After I was more than 28 years of age, I *rode*, as it is termed, with another physician, for some time, before I entered upon the full responsibilities and duties of the medical profession, and I assure you, that to this hour, I have never for one moment regretted it.

LETTER XXIV.

MONEY GETTING.

In a community like our own, where the road to wealth, like the road to market, lies open to all; where every one, for aught which can be foreseen, may become a Girard or an Astor, it is not strange that the love of money should be a predominating trait or element of human character; and of the character of young men as well as old. For young men are older men in miniature, and soon learn to copy them in their employments, habits, virtues, and vices.

Nor is it strange, that in denouncing the love of money as the root of all evil, many worthy individuals should be found, who pass to the extreme of inculcating—what, indeed, they may not themselves always practise—an utter disregard of property. Nay, it is not strange, even, if a few should hold forth, especially to the young, that money is not only to be neglected, but despised.

Now it happens that truth in this matter, as in many others, lies somewhere between extremes. To the old and the young, as a means to an end, or rather as an instrument to an end, money has its value. In truth, there are not a few Christians so low in the scale of moral progress, as not to know that there is a higher or more laudable means of securing the ends they seek, than getting money. They may outgrow this ignorance by and by; if Christians, indeed, they *will* outgrow it. But to say to them as they now are, that the pursuit of wealth, in every degree, and in all circumstances, is morally wrong, would be not merely to check their upward progress, but to put an end to it.

Nature, in the material world, abhors a vacuum; and so of *human* nature. To take away the pursuit of property, or even the love of it, entirely, and at once, would be to take from some men all motive to exertion; and to make their minds and hearts a vacuum.

This is not to deny the general truth of the Scriptures, nor to raise the slightest doubt in regard to their statements on this subject. The love of pleasure—another personage of the world's trinity—is a root of all kinds of evil, as well as the love of money; and yet who is there that would utterly reject it as a motive in human action?

The truth is, we are to do our duty; in doing which, as society is now constituted, money or property will inevitably come. And when received, it is to be taken care of as a means of doing good. It is blessed to receive; but more blessed to communicate or give. Now, such is the usual connection between labor and its reward—work and pay—that most men come insensibly to confound things that may not naturally belong together. Duty is the end; money a means only. Just as it is in regard to seeking happiness.

The great end of human exertion should be holiness. Nevertheless, the general arrangement of things being such that holiness secures happiness, we come to confound them, or to seek both, the latter as well as the former; and sometimes the latter, chiefly, without thinking of the former. Here and every where, let us do our duty and take the consequences.

Let me not be understood as inclining to the opinion of a few eminent men, that the more business a man does, and the more money he gains in being thorough in his business, the better it is even for his spiritual growth. I believe it was Dr. Adam Clark who said, in relation to this subject: "The more irons you have in the fire the better." But this is carrying the matter too far.

Nevertheless it is true—and may every young man who reads this give heed—that God has made you to live in this world, and to do business in it. The road to heaven lies through earth, and, so far as man is concerned, always will. There is, doubtless, such a thing as buying and selling, and getting gain in a lawful manner. There is such a thing as doing business, and receiving the avails of doing business in such a manner as will please God, and in the language of Scripture, glorify him. But there is a more excellent way than that which is commonly pursued, and which has given rise to the prejudices against doing business which have often existed in contemplative minds.

What is this more excellent way? Numerous answers to the question, in a general way, may undoubtedly be given. We may say it is to do as we would be done by. Or, we may say, it is to look on the things of others, as well as on our own. Or, again, that it is to regard not solely our own, but also another's wealth or welfare. Or, again still, it is to glorify God in whatsoever we do. Or, finally, it is to have HOLINESS TO THE LORD written on all we do; our business, of course, not excepted.

Let us, however, be a little more particular. A young man has something to sell, for which he desires, as lawfully he may, an equivalent in money. In such a case, though he is entitled to the full value of the article, yet he must never forget the rights of the person to whom he sells. He is entitled to the full value of his money.

In buying, also, the seller's rights are to be

considered as well as our own. As we are entitled to the full value of our money, so he is entitled to the value, in full, of his property. And we are not only to consider this, but to see that he has it. As Christian young men, we cannot honestly suffer ourselves to come short of this.

Again, in exchanging property, we are to look, every man, on the things and rights of others. True, it often happens in buying and selling, but especially in exchanging property, that both parties may not only have their rights, but one party or the other something more.

A and B, for example, have each a house to live in; but the house of B would better accommodate A than his own does. Or, it may be the reverse; that A's house would better accommodate B than his own. Or, it may be that an exchange, while it secures to each all his just rights, might also give to each something more than the demands of mere justice. In other words, it may happen that one party may gain something without any loss to the other; or, in fewer instances, both may be gainers, and the exchange may make both of them richer.

My opinion is, that no young man should buy, sell, or exchange in such a way that the other party will, as a necessary result, be the loser, unless by his own consent. Nay, I am compelled to go even farther than this—I suppose we are bound to see that every one with whom we deal has his just rights—in other words, we must not suffer him even to defraud himself if we can help it.

Now, as to an equal division of the gains over and above what is required to do strict justice to the party with whom we deal—whether, for example, when by receiving A's house for mine, I not only get the full value of my property, and he the full value of his, but there is a gain to me, by reason of peculiar circumstances, of five hundred dollars, and to him of but two hundred—whether, in such a case, I say, I am bound, as a Christian, to divide equally with him, each receiving three hundred and fifty dollars, or an equivalent for the sum, is quite another question.

There is, however, a higher rule than any I

have mentioned—high at least in appearance, if not in reality—which is to do what we suppose our Saviour would do in our circumstances. And if this consideration should not enable us to decide the question satisfactorily, nothing short of this should.

Here is the grand test for young and old. Hear ye this, young men, and be wise. Get property; but get it as the Lord Jesus Christ would, if placed in your own circumstances; remembering that to this same divine personage you must ere long render an account, not only in the presence of those with whom you have dealt, but in the presence of an assembled universe.

LETTER XXV.

PLEASURE SEEKING.

All seek happiness; and why should they not? They see others in full pursuit after it; they are taught—not merely by Pope, but by better men than he—that happiness is "our being's end and aim." They are even taught that virtue itself "consists in doing good for the sake of everlasting happiness."

They have set up a standard so high and so holy, that few, if any, have, as yet, come up to it. Some have indeed rejected this doctrine theoretically. They have talked of disinterestedness. They have made it synonymous with the love of the gospel.

I am not about to discuss the great question in theology, whether or not disinterested love is our duty. I am not about to oppose even the general pursuit of happiness. Admit, if you please, that the great and good—the great, I mean whose goodness made them so—had respect, in much that they did, to the recompense of reward, as the Scriptures themselves assure us. Admit that no man ought or can turn out of doors the inborn love of happiness which prevails in and prompts, in a greater or less degree, every human breast. But what then? It is one thing to have the love of happiness influence us in a degree, and quite another to suffer it to be the predominating rule of our action.

The young, in particular, I again say, seek for pleasure. Who will show us any good? is in practice their constant cry. Self-denial—the refusal of present pleasure for a higher degree of that which is remote—is to them irksome. Few can be induced to submit to it. And though they suffer from time to time the consequences of their short-sightedness, they still persist. A distant heaven and a distant hell are alike, to them, unmeaning; or, at least, unmoving.

I speak here, however, of those who have

not yet passed from the earlier stages of life to adolescence. I speak not of him who is sixteen, eighteen, or twenty years of age. He ought to know better than to make happiness his being's end and aim. Granted that the great idea held out to him, first at the infant school, and afterwards in the family, and even the Sabbath school, viz., "Be happy," has grown with his growth and strengthened with his strength. Still a higher and less selfish system ought by this time to be inculcated.

Although he should not be taught to despise happiness, or even to forget it, every young man should be told that in order to fulfil the great intention of the Creator, with respect to himself, a predominating aim should be to be good; or, in other words, to be holy.

A venerable minister once said, in the exordium of his discourse, "The great end of Christianity, brethren, is to make men wiser and better." He was thought extravagant; but so was the Saviour when he taught his ultra doctrines on the Mount and elsewhere.

The gospel is for the young as well as the old—the younger the better. Gospel morality, moreover, should be urged on them, as the only true morality—nay, as the only sound morality. And no sounder morality can be inculcated on young men than that which is indicated by the injunction, Labor to be good.

Let this be a predominating motive in all your whole life. Let it influence you at going out and coming in; at your employments, your studies, your recreations; at your lying down, and at your rising up. But on this topic I have spoken at large already.

If it once becomes a great aim of your life to grow wiser and better, you need not longer trouble yourselves about happiness. Enough of this—quite as much as is best for you—will be sure to flow in.

The Saviour's repeated assurance to the good, was, Ye have your reward; not merely, Ye *shall* have it. Your heaven, if you are holy, will begin here; though it will, of course, only begin here. The more holiness, however, the more heaven for you here or hereafter. Happiness, you thus see, is merely a consequence—the child, not the parent of holiness.

But once more. Observe, if you please, that

in speaking of the desire to become good, or holy, as a predominating motive to action, I have said *a*, not *the.* For even this is not the whole of "our being's end and aim." The great end of Christianity is, indeed, to make men wiser and better; but then your great end is not alone to make yourself wiser and better; but also to make wiser and better those around you.

The soundness of the first statement of a venerable and excellent Christian formulary of doctrine—that "man's chief end is to glorify God and enjoy him forever"—if applied to man, individually, may be almost questioned; since the enjoyment of the individual himself, as the idea has been commonly received, is made rather too prominent. It is quite possible that future reflection and future progress in Christian knowledge and experience, may lead to an improvement of the formulary referred to. Perhaps it may yet be said (and with more of truth) that man's chief end is to glorify God by carrying forward, in the highest possible degree, the holiness of himself and of his fellow-creatures.

Do you ask what you can do in the way of advancing the holiness of mankind—and do you say that you are not a missionary, set apart to proclaim the gospel to the world? I reply, in the first place, that you have no right to move a hand, or foot, or finger, without regarding the good of others.

In truth you are not able—such is the condition and constitution of society—to make a single movement, which shall not tend either to advance or retard the well-being of mankind.

And, in the second place, if you *are not* set apart in due form to the work of a missionary—if you *do not* actually hear the command forever sounding in your ears, "Go into all the world, and preach the gospel"—still you are as strongly bound to make yourself and every body else good to the utmost extent of your power, as if it were so.

I wish I could live to see a generation of young men rise up and take the places of their fathers, whose constant aim should be to do every thing in such a manner as should most conduce to public and individual good; or, in other words, to general and individual holiness.

The constant aim to do every thing in the best possible manner wouid lead, almost inevitably, to the full realization of the scriptural promise—He that watereth, shall himself also be watered; and to the blessed results alluded to by the current maxim, Teaching we learn, and giving we retain. But whether I shall live to behold so blessed a period or not, somebody will.

Young men are not apt to care for the good or ill effects of their conduct on others. How frequently do we hear from mouths the expression "I don't care!" For one instance, however, in which we have this expression put into words, it is ten times thought. And yet, this "don't care" spirit, according to the celebrated John Foster, is the very essence of human depravity.

Pleasure-seeking, therefore, as such, should be given up by every considerate and intelligent young man; and he should at once change the object of pursuit. To make himself and every body holy, should be henceforth his great purpose.

In this way, it is true, pleasure would be gained—pleasure of the most exalted kind, too; as greatly different from that short-lived pleasure with which so many of the present generation content themselves, as heaven is different from hell. I speak here as a philosopher, and not as a Christian—aware, however, that on this point the language of philosophy and Christianity is in perfect harmony

Let him who has a desire to do something more in this world than merely to vegetate,—to live a life of mere passivity, like the oyster, rather—give to this important part of my general subject a full measure of his attention. In Scripture language, "He that hath ears to hear, let him hear."

LETTER XXVI.

MENTAL EXCITANTS.

As yet, I have said nothing, or almost nothing, on mental excitants—of which, in every form of civic society, great numbers exist. Let me call your attention for a few moments, to this part of my subject.

It might almost be affirmed, of a community like our own, without any facts before us, other than those which have been presented in my letters on temperance, that it is excessively fond of mental excitants. For, who ever saw an individual whose diseased nervous and digestive systems were constantly crying, Give, give, and yet were never satisfied with plain food, whose intellectual and moral appetites were not as urgent in their demands, and quite as unreasonable?

But, then, we have facts in the greatest abundance. What is the character of our modern libraries—the best of them? I do not allude here, of course, to our circulating libraries, as we generally find them in our large cities, towns, and thoroughfares; for these are well known to be made up of excitable stuff: but, as I remarked before, to the better sort of them. How few solid books, indeed, are published! How few, in fact, of those which possess real worth, are ever read, unless *highly spiced* in some way.

I have sometimes wished for the moment that Boards of Supervision could be established at various points of our wide-spread country, whose office it should be to recommend, if nothing more, such books and such alone, as were deemed suitable for town, social, district, and private libraries.

And then again, I have looked with great pleasure, and with much of hope, to the colporteur and agent system, as a means of gradually supplanting the heterogeneous mass of books which is every where found, in these days, by more substantial materials with which to build up character.

However, there is, and ever will be, one drawback upon the usefulness of such arrangements, even were they effected. It is of comparatively little use to place good and wholesome, but plain food before the young, if they cannot be induced to take it. And such I fear would be the final fate of good books, placed *per force*, before those whose taste is already vitiated. They would not be read; or if read, they would not be relished.

I do not forget that I have spoken to you before, on the subject of *light* reading. But there is a worse class of books and papers before the young in these days, than light ones; since a book may be light, and yet not greatly exciting. Even our newspapers, magazines and pamphlets might be of a much better character in this respect, than some of them now are. They might be light, and yet healthy.

A large proportion of our novels, especially those published first in our catch-penny papers or magazines, and afterwards thrown out, in pamphlet form, in miserable type, upon still worse paper, and sold *cheap*, are of the exciting class. Indeed, they are *intended* to be exciting, just as much as pies and cakes, and sweetmeats, and confectionery, are intended to be so! It is because they are so, that they obtain so ready a sale.

I will even venture the assertion, now that we are at the place for it, that it is precisely to those who have been trained up to pies, pastry and confectionery, that these paltry productions of a licentious press are particularly adapted, and that it is they who, in greatest numbers, fall victims to their influence.

I use the word licentious, however, in a more general sense, in this place, than is customary. But I might go further and speak of the press as being licentious to a very great extent, in a more particular and local point of view. For is it not strictly true that a very large proportion of these publications prove exciting *because* they are licentious; and that, too, in the very worst sense of the word? I know well that their licentiousness may not—

in fact, *does* not—always appear externally; but in this covered, or at least half-concealed condition, is it not so much the more dangerous?

There is even a graver class of books than those to which I have here alluded, that are far too exciting for the healthy mental palate. This class is to be found in our bookstores. I scarcely know a man who would hesitate to keep and sell them, even though he were a professed disciple of the Saviour.

This may seem a very grave charge, but is it not founded on the strictest truth? It is not asserted, or even intimated, that these men who sell the machinery of Satan, ever consider well what they are doing. They are trained to it—they act as mere machines, or almost so. If you say they have no right thus to act—they are bound to reflect—my reply is, *that* is your own assertion, and not mine. To their own master they stand or fall, who deal out to the community, in any way or shape, what operates like a fire-brand every where, whether it acts upon the body, the mind, or the heart. Nor does it mend their condition very much to be able to say in the great day of account, that they did it in sport, or even to obtain a livelihood.

But you may, perhaps, regard this as a digression. Be it so. Before we return, however, let me give you one or two cautions.

Should you be so fortunate as to escape the deteriorating influences of the whole paraphernalia of physical, intellectual, and moral excitement; and should the temptation present itself of spreading before the public, as a means of gaining a subsistence for yourself and family, such things as I have referred to, remember that you are not now in the condition of those whose minds have never been at all enlightened on this subject. Weigh well the consequences of your conduct, before you act. Remember your accountability to God, and to future generations.

Again, should you be placed, in the arrangements of the Divine Providence, at the head of a family, remember that he who in his wisdom seemed to *concentrate all* wisdom, when he said, "Train up a child in the way he should go, and when he is old he will not depart from it"—enjoyed the very best of opportunities for knowing the tendency of an overfondness for physical excitement, to awaken and feed the fire (already raging within), of the appetites and passions. Remember, I say, and beware!

I have before intimated, that I hardly know what to advise a young man, in regard to exciting books, except to steer clear of them all. He has not the power, if he had the disposition, to burn up all the volumes in the Christian world, as Omar (I believe it was he) did in the Mohammedan. Nor would he accomplish his purpose of ridding the world of them, if he did. Like the fabled Phœnix, others just like them would rise from their ashes. Worse than this, perhaps, would happen. Like the exorcised man in the gospel—seven spirits more wicked than the first would be substituted.

Besides, such a conflagration is by no means desirable. Amid the books, magazines and papers, which have come up among us, like the frogs upon Egypt, we have many that are excellent. A young man is not obliged to buy or read Bulwer, Byron and Eugene Sue, because he finds them in a bookstore kept by a good man, or because he sees others buy and read them. He may deny himself in this particular, as well as in many others.

No cross, no crown, was a maxim of Penn, and a wise one. I am not at all certain that He who continually brings good out of evil, and causes even the wrath of man to praise him, may not have it in contemplation to raise up a better class of men and women than the world has yet seen, by means of these very excitements of which I have been speaking in this letter; I mean now, indirectly. For if it be true, that without cross, there is no crown; then is it not also true, that the greater the cross, the greater the crown, provided it be well sustained!

Let him, therefore, who in the arrangements of the family to which he belongs, is placed at a table where excitants abound, remember that this is his trial—his cross. Here may be, at the least, the very lessons which, if properly studied, are to teach him the way of self-denial and self-renunciation. How can a person be expected to deny himself and take up his cross, in the larger, less frequently recurring affairs of life, who has not first learned to deny himself in small matters?

The same remarks and the same admonition may apply to the case of those before whom exciting intellectual and moral food is continually presented. If they govern the appetite—which incessantly cries, Give, give—in these smaller occurrences, may they not hope to pave the way for self-government in larger matters, whenever the time of trial shall come?

We need not, therefore, to pray to our Father in Heaven, that he would take our young men out of the world, in order that they may be what he designed they should be; but only that he will keep them from its evils. And suiting the action to the word, as we should pray, so we should labor. Our young men must soon be old ones; let the desire and prayer of the heart, and the labor of the hands, have such a tendency that they may better sustain the burdens of society and glorify God, than their fathers have done. For until each generation shall be as an improved edition of that which precedes it, the work of God, delegated to man on earth, will never be accomplished.

LETTER XXVII.

RESPECT FOR AGE.

I REMEMBER, well, the time when the young rose up before the aged, whether their age was honorable or otherwise. They did not stay to inquire about their merit; it was sufficient that they were gray-headed.

The rule was, in families, to avoid going between older persons and the fireplace, around which, in a sort of semicircle, the family were often ranged. Or if it became necessary to pass before older persons, in these circumstances, they were to make obeisance to them. This, I say, was the rule—that it was not always rigidly adhered to, does not alter the matter of fact.

On leaving the room, even though none but

our friends were present, obeisance was again required; and so also on returning. If a child or youth passed an older person, or—what was indeed the same thing—if another person passed by him, he was expected and required to bow to him most respectfully and profoundly. Not however till the head was uncovered.

I have seen well nigh half a hundred school pupils range themselves—as it were instinctively, and even instantly—in a row, as an individual a little older than themselves approached their play-ground. And I have seen this long row, with hat or bonnet in hand, so far as hats and bonnets were in use among them, make one simultaneous bow and courtesy to the passer by—no doubt as much to their own satisfaction, as to his personal exaltation.

At the schoo -room too, in those days, no pupil was accustomed to receive any thing at the hands of a teacher or his assistant, without a most reverent and unqualified obeisance. So on coming into the school-room, whether at the opening of the school or at recess; and so also, at all times, and in all circumstances, when in the act of leaving it.

Nor was this all. At table, if indeed the young sat at the table with those who were older, (which was not always permitted,) the former, unless spoken to, were expected to be silent. If they wanted any thing, however, they might ask for it; but the request was to be accompanied, or rather prefaced by a Please Sir, or Please Ma'am.

Especially was youth required to bow low —not to say fawn and creep—before age invested with power or dignity, whether or not that power and dignity were well used. In some of our higher seminaries it would have been thought criminal, indeed absolutely rebellious, not to take off the hat, and retain it in hand while the professor or tutor was passing; and many a reprimand, if not actual expulsion, has grown out of delinquencies of this same general character.

And once more. All the customs of our social circles, festive boards, public amusements, and arrangements for divine worship, were based on the broad principle that respect should and must be rendered by the young to the old. The arm-chair and the stool and cricket, the more elevated seat and the mere slab bench, the high bed and the trundle bed, the body of the church and the gallery—these, and many more things which could be named in the same connection, all looked the same way. Even the congregation at church was seated with sole reference to age. The aged fathers and mothers were seated nearest the deacons' pew and the pulpit, while the rest were placed nearer or more remote from the last, according as they were nearer or more remote from them in years.

Such a thing as seating a congregation on any other principle was not known, in the region of New England where I was brought up, till within fifty years. No gray-headed man, because he was poor, was forced to sit remote from the preacher, in some dark corner, where, from his growing infirmities, he could scarcely hear what was said to him. The gospel, in those days, was for the poor, as well as for the rich, just as its Author intended it.

Yet, while I would commend, even with

warmth, some of the forms of showing respect for the aged which prevailed half a century ago, I would not be understood as seeming to endorse them all. I would not carry the custom of making bows and courtesies, in family or in school, to an extreme which savors of tithing the mint and cummin, while the weightier matters are omitted. I would not require the young to be so scrupulous about "manners," during the hours of study, labor, or recreation, as to defeat the great ends for which these things were designed.

Why should the young, during the school recess, while busy at their plays, (as necessary to them as their graver studies,) be compelled to arrange themselves in rows to make obeisance to the passing stranger? Why should they, even, be expected to stop their amusements at all? Why take any notice of the passer by, except to see that they do not obstruct his way?

True it is, that if spoken to, I would have them reply, and add thereto a movement of the head, especially if the person who speaks to them is greatly their superior in point of years.

And if children, at school or at home, stand gazing at the traveller as he passes, it is but reasonable that they should make their obeisance to him.

Perhaps it is unnecessary, in a letter to young men, to be thus minute in regard to the duty of the mere schoolboy. Let it be remembered, however, that I am merely endeavoring to illustrate the principles I would inculcate. I wish to leave the general impression, that mankind every where, and in all ages, are prone to extremes—in avoiding one rock of error, apt to run on another. The customs of our ancestors were founded in truth, only they carried them to an unwise extreme.

And yet, in departing from the extreme into which they fell, have we not gone into an opposite extreme still less wise, and still more unjustifiable? Is it reasonable for the young, so generally, to place themselves on a level with the old? Is it reasonable that they should assume that wisdom and experience, which, if they do not always accompany age, are never to be acquired without it?

Is it reasonable that the young should take

to themselves the right of occupying the best seats, where a choice is to be had; whether at home, or abroad; whether at church or at the concert, and whether the occasion be grave or solemn? Have we not gospel rules—examples rather—from which the wise young man may receive timely hints for the government of his conduct in this matter? What, then, are we to learn from the earnest injunction not to take the highest seats at weddings, feasts, &c.? Shall youth claim a right, in the presence and company of the aged, which even the gospel of the Lord Jesus Christ, republican as it is—I had almost said, ultra republican—does not concede to those who are older, in the presence of their supposed equals?

The question will perhaps be asked—But what shall we do, when age lays claim to superiority—and makes large claims, too? Shall the young be expected to concede all that the old may arbitrarily desire?

Such a question is a pertinent one. I have seen age make very unreasonable claims. Old men are not always wise. I have seen children compelled to sit for an hour or two, when they were quite uncomfortable, that age might not be disturbed in its follies—when it would have been equally happy, had it yielded a little more liberty to those over whom Providence had given it unlimited control.

Yet, after all, the general demand, both of reason and revelation, is, submission;—I mean, to the higher authority. The powers that be, in the family at the least, are ordained by God. If by mild and gentle expostulation, or even by respectful request, I could not gain what I conceived to be my rights, I would yield them, at once. Better to suffer, in well-doing, than be guilty of evil-doing. Is it not so?

These collisions, moreover, to which I now refer—to which, indeed, all the remarks of this chapter refer—take place at an age when young persons are more likely to mistake concerning their own rights than at any other. This shall be my principal apology for dwelling a few moments longer on so important a subject.

As the individual passes from boyhood to youth, and from youth to manhood, his size increases faster than his experience. He is more a man physically, than he is intellectually and morally. He is not, as yet—say at fourteen or fifteen—wise enough to know that size and strength are not the standard by which he is to be measured, and by which he ought not to measure himself. He has fallen into the mistaken notion that old folks, generally, are fools, and that as each successive generation, collectively, is wiser than that which preceded it, so he is wiser than the generation next before him. A remark this is, however, which I have made in another letter.

This mistake, so common with young men, is most influential at precisely the period of life when it is most dangerous. Were it to be made while they are very young, it would be less hurtful; or were it deferred to a period which brings with it a little more experience and a great deal more humility, it would also prove comparatively harmless. Or at least, coming at either of these seasons, it would not so often result in abuses and excesses. It would be palliated, in its effects, by other circumstances.

There is a period in every young man's

history, when dangers of every kind thicken around him, and seem to threaten inevitable destruction. I allude, of course, to the stormy period when we are said to pass the Terra del Fuego of life's journey. And such is the violence, to most, of the storms that assail at this critical period, that we are not to wonder if thousands and millions of our race are left to suffer, under their influence and their own inexperience, a most fatal and terrible shipwreck.

For it is not a little remarkable, that just at this time, when all other restraints begin to lose their hold on a young man, the passions not only rage with most violence, but are most unwilling to brook the least restraint. The same is true of all the appetites. Were parental influence growing stronger at this juncture, or were that influence which is exerted by good and virtuous sisters on the increase at this time, the state of things to which I refer would be less unhappy.

But, alas! no father, or mother, or brother, or sister, can, at this dangerous hour, do much to lessen the dangers that so terribly threaten.

Parents are fools, and sisters weak, in the estimation of young men. All wisdom, or almost all, seems bestowed by Heaven just to make bright and glorious their own happy pathway; and to die with them, for aught they know or care, when their own mortal journey is completed!

There is but one condition of things—extraneous to the reason and good sense of the young man himself—that can do much to lessen the danger, at this time, of making a most fatal shipwreck. Blessed be God, who in his wise Providence has ordained that a new bond of attachment should spring up, just now, to save from absolute, inevitable, and irretrievable destruction.

I do not say that this bond always holds, as with an omnipotent power. Yet I do say, that, besides it, none but Omnipotence can restrain us. It is not John Newton* alone that has

* Most of my readers doubtless know that Mr. Newton was early employed in the slave trade to Africa, and, by the force of the storm within and the temptation without, was often in danger. Having formed an early and abiding attachment, however, this bond, as an anchor, held him. The

felt the restraint; but every son of Adam, who has reached the age of puberty and witnessed the results accomplished by puberty on those around him. And if the mighty cord has not wholly held him to the paths of purity, it has done all it could. What he is, he owes, under God, to what it has done. But on this and several kindred topics I hope to have room to enlarge on another occasion.

Happy the young man who, at the dangerous Terra del Fuego of human life, avails himself of every help which God in Providence and nature has proffered him. Let him set his sails for every needed pilot, and let him give due heed to every needful and available monitor, whether internal or external.

Young men need counsel at every period and hour of their existence—but most of all, at that perilous season when the necessity is least perceived. Let them keep hold of the parent's arm here, if nowhere else. Let female influence be felt here, if nowhere else. Let conscience utter her monitory voice here,

thought, What would she think of me, if I yield to indiscretion? often, as he says, saved him.

if nowhere else; and here, at this precise point—the point of danger—let her voice be heard and heeded. Nor let the voice of him whose mandates are higher than conscience be overlooked or forgotten.

But I am anticipating. My business just now is, to encourage in the young a due respect for the aged; especially at a period when such respect seems to be, in the common course of things, almost obliterated. It is not true that respect for the old—the disposition to consider yourself as second to him—is only becoming while you are in the merest childhood and infancy. It is becoming always. It is not only becoming—it is a virtue. It is as pleasing to God as it is acceptable to man.

One thought more on this topic, and I will close this long letter. Respect for age will never lower your reputation among your equals. Some young men there are who think or seem to think it such a mark of weakness to respect age that they have not the moral courage to do that which they would otherwise think, in the nature of things, perfectly right. Now I will not deny that there are individuals to be found, with whom they will lose something by respecting and reverencing the old. They take the highest place—age or no age—and others may take care of themselves. But let not the young be deceived. These very individuals know better than they say, all the while. They may laugh at you outwardly, but they cannot help respecting you inwardly. Or if they contrive to brave it through to the end of life, a day is coming when they will view the matter very differently—a day when, in the presence of assembled worlds, they will not be slow to confess that, though honorable age may not always be that which standeth in multitude of years, yet *age*, whether honorable or dishonorable, is to be respected and cherished. You have read the story of Fidelia—who, though one of the most accomplished women of her age, devoted herself to her aged father; and felt most at home, not in treating him with a want of due respect, but with all those little attentions which his age required—even putting on his slippers. Go and do thou likewise.

LETTER XXVIII.

DUTIES TO THE AGED.

THE remarks made at the close of my last letter concerning Fidelia, remind me of the duties of the young to the aged, especially to their own parents. These are numerous and weighty.

It is by no means sufficient to have a general respect for those who are older than ourselves, though without this no young man is well fitted for the journey of life. We should have more than a general respect for them;—they must be nourished and cherished—as in our own bosoms. Precious beyond all price are these relics of a gone-by generation, even though connected to us by no ties of blood.

For has it never occurred to you in your search for happiness—for the young are exceedingly active in this search—has it never occurred to you, I say, that, instead of satisfying yourself with merely treating age with a sort of general respect as matter of duty, such treatment should be one of your highest pleasures—a thing which involves some of your highest and most important interests?

You have heard of the love of Jacob for his grandchildren as well as for his children—and are not ignorant that the lives of the old are as it were bound up in those of the young. Nay, you must have often observed this trait of old age, in those who are around you. But is there to be no reciprocation of feeling? Do the old love the young, with a love that is unquenchable, and have the young no love for the old? Is there nothing to be done on their part, but to show them a cold, or at most a lukewarm respect? Has God so ordered it?

An aged domestic animal may be turned aside, when no longer useful, and the owner incur no guilt. Such, at least, is the stern decree of society. But can humanity, in its decline, be thus treated, and the agent of its cruel neglect be blameless? Can it be so, in the nature of things?

Can the young even approximate to such a course and be blameless? Yet what son is there among us who does not thus approximate? Who—where is he that comes up to the full measure of the great command of God which requires us to honor age, especially in our aged parents?

If I understand, correctly, the duties of the young towards the aged — the aged parent more particularly—they are all comprised in a few words. The general injunction might be framed thus: In all the circumstances of your lives, so conduct as to make the most of your parents—their health, reputation, virtue, talents, piety, &c.—and this in their hundredth year no less than in their fiftieth.

Did not Fidelia's reputation rise at every thing she did to make the most of an aged and decrepit parent? Bad as the world is, it cannot resist the claims of filial piety. He who labors, in season and out of season, to husband the waning resources of a declining ancestor, is laboring with most of efficiency to advance his own reputation, even though he were acting solely on selfish principles.

I have seen a young man who, as his parents advanced along the decline of life, seemed to think it for his interest to hide them from society. They might, indeed, be well fed and clothed—properly foddered, as one might say; but this was all he cared for. And even this supply for the wants of their bodies might have been bestowed grudgingly, but for the selfish fear of losing reputation by it.

I have seen this same young man, with a view to place himself in the foreground, and throw his aged parents into obscurity, contrive to remove them from the home of their whole lives—from the cradle to seventy—that he might occupy the mansion himself, and consign them to a small tenement in a retired part of the village, where they could scarcely see or be seen, at least by any but the authors of their exile; nor by them as long as inclination or interest called them in another direction.

I have known the same young man proceed a step farther, and having fairly ejected both parents from their much-loved mansion and long-cherished home, dwell with so much and such frequent interest on the benefits likely to result to himself from their decease, as actually to express a willingness to have them out of the way; or, as he said, to have them freed from their trials and troubles and infirmities.

Now, can it be possible that such a young man has any right views of his duties to the aged—especially to aged parents? What! bound to make the most of them at every step of life, and yet practically make the least of them he possibly can?

Does he not know they love the young? That they live much in the past, and take much delight in repeating the past? That in order to dwell much in the past, they must have constant access to that other extreme of society, that lives and delights to live almost wholly in the future? For the love of story-telling is not stronger in the old than the love to hear stories is in the young, and God made the two to go together. And what God has joined together, will man presume to put asunder?

Besides, the old are more healthy, much more so, in the society of the young. They need the stimulus of that society, much more than when they were in active life. Then, their minds were occupied. They were buying and selling, marrying or giving in marriage. They had something before them. Now all these things are over with them; especially when banished from the world to a corner of a field, or some other secluded spot.

Let me entreat you, my young friends, to make such arrangements as shall keep your aged parents in the society of one or another—several, if possible—of their children. It is a duty you owe to them; but it is much more: it is a duty you owe to yourselves. They have acquired a vast amount of experience which they have not yet learned to transmit on paper, but which will be of inestimable worth to you, if you can obtain it. Now by enjoying their society, and giving them an opportunity to enjoy yours, you will afford them an opportunity, from time to time, to bring out, in the form of stories, as I have already said, just that sort of information which you and your children need, and in just the right shape.

It is sometimes said that the old cannot be connected with the families of their children without exercising that freedom which often results in a degree of uneasiness—to call it by a name no worse—about the children. All this I understand, most fully. But they need not be in the same family with the young in every particular, nor even in the same house. They may retain—it is better that they should—the old mansion, and you may build near them. We do not hear of any quarrel between the families of Jacob and Joseph on account of Joseph's children.

I have not yet mentioned one highly important reason why the young should make as much as possible of the old. It is, that they may have the full benefit of their judgment in matters of business, &c. For, though the young are apt to think they know more than the old when they are at fifteen, they find out their mistake at twenty, or twenty-five; and that advice and guidance — and above all that authority — which they would have slighted then, they will now receive with thankfulness—and will even solicit it.

Startle not at the word authority, which has just been used. It is only in the earliest years of life that the parent should be an autocrat in his family. In subsequent years, his commands must be such as will commend themselves to the free agency of those for whom they are designed. But this species of authority does not cease—or rather should not—at exactly twenty-one, as too many suppose. The same species of authority which is proper at sixteen, is proper at twenty-one; and that which is really needful at twenty-one, does not entirely cease to be necessary at twenty-two, or twenty-five, or even thirty. In truth, it remains as long as the parties remain in existence.

But if parental authority, though it may slightly wane, should not cease but with the last pulsation of parental life, then it follows, of course, that obedience, on the part of the young, ought not to cease at an earlier period. Authority on the one part implies submission on the other, and of course cannot exist without it.

Such views as these—in these days of pseudo republicanism—may not, I know, be very popular. But I have another thing to aim at in these letters besides being popular. I am to state the truth, according to my views of it, without fear of losing favor, as well as without an overweening desire to receive it. The truth is, that insubordination has been the order of the day, in these United States, and even in this land of the Puritans; and the whole length and breadth of society are infected by it. And it is almost as much as a man's reputation is worth to set himself against it. Nor will subordination be very soon restored, unless it can be done through the medium of the family and the school; for the genius of our government tends to perpetuate it.

LETTER XXIX.

POLITICS AND POLITICAL DUTIES.

WHILE the young need information at almost every step of life, I know of few things in regard to which counsel is more needed—the counsel of old men, even—than on the subject of their political conduct and duties.

Mankind, young and old, are so constituted as to be prone to extremes. In departing from Scylla, they are apt to fall on Charybdis. This is especially the case in the matter of politics.

Here is a young man, for example, scarcely in his teens, who knows more, in his own estimation, by one half, than his neighbors of thirty, forty, and fifty. He can discuss with unblushing boldness the merits of all our presidential and gubernatorial candidates. He knows *because* he knows, and if he can render no reason it makes little difference to himself.

The modest young man, disgusted with his blustering, goes to the opposite extreme, and declares, in haste, that he will have nothing to do with politics; and ten to one but he carries his threat into execution. He falls as far short of the true course as the other goes beyond it.

Or, it may happen occasionally, that the blustering politician of twelve or fifteen may himself become disgusted, and fall upon the opposite extreme. Such things have come under my observation during the last fifty years, and may not have escaped the observation of others.

One reason why young men move in this way—that is, run from one extreme to another—is that they have no conscience in the matter, and no good reason for supposing that others have. They take up their opinions either upon trust, or by chance, and they hold and profess them as a mere matter of convenience or amusement. In short, to them, politics is little more than a game, into which they as little think of carrying any thing in the shape of conscience, as to a billiard-table or a checker-board.

Need I say to the intelligent young men of our own intelligent republic, that all this is wrong? Need I remind you of the great truth so often and so earnestly insisted on by Paul, that whether we eat or drink, or whatsoever we do, we are bound to do all to the glory of God? This is, indeed, a rule for Christians; but am I writing for any other? Is there a young man who reads one of my letters through, who does not acknowledge the divine authority of Christianity?

To do a thing to the glory of God, is to do it in such a manner as will be acceptable to him. It is to perform it as a matter of duty—not *without*, but *with* a conscience. I entreat you to remember this. Whatever is worth doing in this world, is worth doing well. But to do a thing well, we must regard ourselves as under obligations to high heaven to do it right—that is, conscientiously.

You are to attend to your political duties in the fear of God, and with a sense of accountability to him for the manner in which you discharge them, just as much as you are to go to church in this way. But on this point do not misunderstand me. I am not placing your duties to God and those to your fellow-men on a par with each other. I have not the remotest thought of doing so. All I mean to say is, that duty is as truly duty in the one case as in the other. It may be higher in the one case than in the other—indeed, it is so—but then both are equally duty; and, in their respective places, equally binding.

But if the duties we owe to our fellow-beings in the shape of political duties are to be thus sacredly regarded, then it follows that they are matters about which every young man ought to be enlightened. He ought not to be permitted to grow to manhood in almost utter ignorance of this whole subject. And yet such is the unhappy condition of most of our American young men!

This word American, to my own apprehension, speaks volumes. Young men of America —free, enlightened, and comparatively happy America—is it to you that I am permitted thus to write? Exalted privilege! may it never be abused. And may you never, in the plenitude of your freedom, find yourselves disposed to make light of those counsels which, though they come from age, are yet warm from a heart that age has not yet chilled or contracted.

You are bound to make yourselves acquainted—familiarly so—with the geography and history of your own country. Is it said, that at the present day, every one is thus instructed? Not so fast. The great majority of our young men know almost nothing, practically, about either. They may have recited at the schools on both. But their recitations have been, for the most part, mere parrot work. They were words of others, and not ideas of their own.

Some of you may be inclined to ask what this thorough knowledge of the geography and history of one's own country has to do with the proper and conscientious discharge of our political duties. It has every thing to do with it. Why do you take a deeper interest in the welfare of places you have resided in, or seen, than in places which you never saw, and of which you have a very faint, or very crude conception? Why would you sooner defend them? Is it not because they are to you realities?

Then become familiarly acquainted with the whole country of which you are an inhabitant, that all parts of it, and the interests of all parts will be realities to you.

There is as great a difference between two young men at the ballot-box—or in the battle-field, even, if battle-field there must be—one of whom is thoroughly and practically a geographer, and the other grossly ignorant on this whole subject, as can possibly be conceived. The former is far more ready to have a due regard to the rights of those who are to be affected by his conduct or his vote, than the latter. Nor is he as readily influenced unduly by the example or persuasion of others. He cannot as readily be bought and sold.

Mankind, unintelligent and unprincipled, are very much like the herding animals. They do this or that because others do it, and not because it is right. They are thinking—if they think at all—of their responsibility to those around them, and not of their responsibility to conscience and to God. They are far more likely to ask, What will others say, than What does God say? or Is it right?

They go where their own clan, or party, or sect, or neighborhood are going. If they do not go to the polls at all, believing it to be a matter of no consequence, many a young man follows their example. If they go for a particular candidate or measure, it is sufficient, they seem to say, if they do the same. If they go to destruction, the young man who is uninstructed and unprincipled will be apt to go with them.

But in proportion as a young man can be made to acquaint himself with the geography and history of his own country—especially such a country as ours—he will be apt to take an interest in its true welfare, not only as a whole, but as composed of various and numerous parts. True, this is not all which is required of him. He must study the constitution and laws of his country. I do not mean to say he must devote his life to this study, for that were impracticable, except his object were to become a lawyer, a jurist, or a statesman.

Nor are these things all. Every young man is under obligation to understand well the customs, habits, manners, and institutions of his country. Travelling is indeed greatly useful for this latter purpose; but then there are substitutes for this. Others have travelled for us, and have given us the results of their observation and reflections. And since no one young man can do every thing, you will act the wise part in consulting the best of our authorities on the subject.

Do not tell me you have no time for making yourself acquainted with the matters to which I have referred; for it is not so. You may not, I am well aware, have as much time to spare as might seem desirable. And yet you have time enough to learn how to perform your duty.

God is not a hard master—gathering where he has not strewed—he requires nothing of you in the way of duty, but what you have time and ability to do. If he has given you the right of suffrage, and required you to exercise it under the light of the nineteenth century, and under the genius of institutions and constitutions like our own, he has given you time to study those institutions and constitutions.

As one of your duties, in this life, you are to

"redeem your time." Now how much time have you hitherto suffered to run to waste in reading which was wholly useless, and in conversation which was equally so? Understand me, however. I am a friend to conversation as a means of improvement, as well as to reading. But then there is not a little time spent in conversation which amounts to just nothing at all, except to amuse.

Such is most of the common conversation on petty and party politics, of which so many young men are excessively fond. It does not qualify them in the slightest degree for the performance of their duties as the free citizens of a free country. Time thus spent—I repeat it—ought to be redeemed.

Nor is it to be redeemed by reading, any more than by conversing on the little and be-littling things to which I have alluded, and which fill so many of the columns of our newspapers in these days. It will require the efforts of more than one generation of young men who shall be true to themselves, their country, and their God, to remove the evils which those pests of society—worse than the scourges of ancient Egypt—have inflicted on our land. They have not only pandered to a miserable taste, but they have created such a taste where it did not before exist.

How can a true friend of his country repress the emotions which are roused by the consideration of the abuses which have been heaped upon us by—not the freedom of expression, but —the licentiousness, and lightness, and sophistry, even, of some of these publications. Need I urge you to shun their corrupting portions and parts, as you would shun the plague or the cholera, and to redeem your time because the days are evil?

LETTER XXX.

FEMALE SOCIETY

THE Author of the world we live in might, for aught we know, have arranged things very differently. Instead of giving but one globe to eight hundred or a thousand millions of our race, he might have divided this larger globe into a thousand million smaller ones, and assigned one of these to each individual.

Then, again, instead of making provision for successive generations of his creatures, he might have formed them on the solitary plan, and allowed them to live on, 'sole monarch' each of his own domain, for thousands—perhaps, thousands of millions—of years.

But such is not the Divine arrangement—such, in our own terrestrial sphere, it never will be. The decree has gone forth from the council chamber of the Eternal; It is not good for man to be alone. It is not good for man individually—it is not good for him collectively. The sum total of human happiness, no less than of human usefulness, would be greatly diminished if all mankind—whether of one sex or two—were to live hermits.

Hence the necessity of the conjugal relation, whose office is twofold—to complete the education of the parties themselves, and to be the means of human progress and improvement through another generation. Hence it is that man shall leave father and mother and cleave to his wife, and that the bond shall not only be as strong as life itself, but as permanent. Hence, in one word, the family and the family state.

Man, divinely appointed to be a social and not a solitary being, begins his career in the family. Were it possible for him to be cast forth on the wide world, like Caspar Hauser, and yet survive, he would be but the mere fragment of a being, and that fragment an almost useless one. Rough, rude, boisterous, and in one word but half-civilized—hewn, but not polished—he would very imperfectly fulfil his high destinies. It is not good for him to be without the pale of female influence, and hence he has been subjected to it.

Few young men have any idea—the most faint or remote—how much they owe to the influence of mothers and sisters, especially the former. Young men at the best. and under the best influences, are often coarse, passionate, sensual—what then would they have been without maternal and sisterly influence? If now, so often, they burst those bonds which should "make man mild and sociable to man," what would they be and do, if those bonds were weaker than now, or above all if they had never existed?

The influence, mutually, of brothers and sisters is wonderful. From the days of Cain, who was set over Abel to influence and to guide him, down to the present moment, the stronger and more masculine have been appointed of heaven to rule over, by a wise and just influence, the feebler and more feminine.

Nor is the influence wholly on the side of the more powerful sex. There is a reciprocation, and more than a reciprocation. Female influence—that of the weaker party—and precisely for this reason that it is female influence, is even stronger than any other.

Brothers, then, I say again, little know how much they owe to the influence of sisters. They would better know—though the experience might be a sad one—had not the Divine mind planned the arrangement which we see of nearly an equal number of brothers and sisters in each family. At least the exceptions to this rule are so few as to constitute nothing more than exceptions. Dr. Rush used to ask those young patients who came to him with a bodily constitution well nigh ruined, if they had sisters.

Despise not, then, O ye young men—as some of you affect to do—the other and weaker sex. Remember they are all sisters—sisters of somebody whom they influence. Nay, more than this, learn to esteem and love them. Lower them not, by word, look, deed, or thought, in their own estimation.

On the contrary, do all in your power to increase rather than diminish their respect for themselves, for so shall you take the most direct course to elevate your own sex.

What if you are not brothers and sisters under the same father and mother? You are still brethren and sisters of the same great family, whose members, from East to West, and from pole to pole, have one common interest. You are in an important sense the children of the same Heavenly Father.

What can be a more lovely sight than that of brothers and sisters who truly love one another, and who seek to elevate, adorn and improve each other? The sight is the more interesting from the fact that the licentious notions of Byron have been so frequently swallowed by the young. They have heard that every woman is at heart a rake, or something worse, till they have been almost led to look with suspicion on their own sisters.

Happy those who have learned that the reverse of what is implied in the slander of Byron were more true. For except in those rare cases where the old adage that "a shameless woman is the worst of men" becomes applicable, woman is by nature not only less rākish, but much purer than man.

I have inquired, what can be more lovely than the sight of loving brothers and sisters under the same roof. But there is a sight still more interesting than even this. It is the sight of those who have bound themselves together, in the love and fear of the great Jehovah, for life.

The former attachment partakes largely—it is inevitable—of the instinctive; the latter is more closely allied to heaven and divine things. The former is apt to wane, as life passes on; the latter ought to increase; and if what it ought to be, does increase till life's termination.

It is one of the most curious of all the Divine arrangements for social life—this new attachment of mankind to each other—precisely at the time and under the circumstances which so imperiously require it. For what would become of you, O young man! if it were so that just at the precise period when deprived of maternal and sisterly influence, and endowed with new and strong passions and appetites, you were to be cut asunder forever from the soft and tender ties which have hitherto bound you? In passing the Terra del Fuego of human life who shall be your pilot? Must you not experience a most dangerous and fatal shipwreck?

And yet, just at this critical moment of your life—this hour of great moral and social peril—behold a new and tender passion springing up, unlike that which bound you to the family circle, and yet in many respects more important. Who is so blind as not to see, in this part of the Divine arrangement, the most boundless wisdom and the most infinite love?

And, if susceptible of gratitude at all, in whose heart does not gratitude spring up, while he contemplates this amazing proof that a Father is at the helm of the universe, "educing good from ill," and blessing all who refuse not the blessing?

And now will any young man, whose heart is not like the nether millstone, permit himself to eye askance, and above all with disdain, that sex which was so manifestly designed in the good providence of God, not only to save him from perdition, but to lift him to the dignity of his real nature?

You love your mothers and sisters; be exhorted then to show your love to them, by securing in your own time and God's, such influences as shall carry out and perfect the great work which your mothers and sisters have begun. In one word, seek the companionship of one who shall prove to you more than mother and sister both, and that for life.

You will not have to live to the age of fifty years, in the present aspect of society and things, (as some of your predecessors have been compelled to do,) before you can spell out the true philosophy of society, and the true ends of conjugal life. God is showing the nations of the earth—and you cannot shut your eyes to the great lesson—that the world's true advancement is to be brought about chiefly by means of individual, family, and neighborhood or church improvement.

Governments have no power—the best of them—to reform mankind and hasten the latter day glory. Their power is always in proportion—as regards both quantity and quality—to individual and family elevation. It is so every where; but it is especially so in our own country

LETTER XXXI.

GENERAL DUTY OF MARRIAGE.

In my last letter, I promised you something more on the great subject to which I then called your attention. My present purpose is to redeem, in part at least, the pledge there given.

I have more than intimated in that letter, that matrimony is a duty, and I mean so. It should be regarded as such by both sexes, but especially by our own. It is a divine ordinance—as old almost as the creation. If order is heaven's first law, as Pope says, it does not seem to be earth's. The first *general* law here is, that man shall "leave father and mother, and cleave to his wife."

The Scriptures do not say, I grant, that

marriage shall take place at twenty or twenty-five, or thirty, or at any particular age. The general rule, I again affirm, is, that we shall marry. Like other general rules, however, it may, nay *must* admit of exceptions. Some there are, no doubt, that ought not to marry, on account of health. And there may be other circumstances in operation, for a time at least, equally imperative.

I would not lay so much stress on this point—the duty of the young to "lay their course" for marriage, were it not that some very excellent persons of both sexes have stoutly denied the doctrine, and insisted that if we are free to do as we please in any thing, it is here. Now, I do not deny that we are *free*, even to do wrong. The Creator has never as yet made a decree for man that hinders him from doing what he pleases—probably he never will. We may, if we choose, refrain from eating and drinking, and starve ourselves to death, but starvation, we may be sure, forms no part of the plan of the Creator. He made us to eat and drink, and live. So also, he made us for matrimony.

The motives to this duty, strong as they may be, are none too powerful. Appetite, affection, passion, ambition, fancy—all of them seem to be needed. They seem intended by the Creator. Not, of course, to rule; but to have a subordinate place. Nor should they be too excitable.

There is a wide difference between strength and excitability—and generally, in the case before us, they are in an inverse proportion to each other. In plain terms, the greater the excitability, the feebler the appetites and passions; and the greater the strength, on the contrary, the less the excitability.

For notwithstanding the whole array of motives to this duty of matrimony, we see thousands and millions in the Old World, and quite too many in the New, who set themselves against it. In some of our cities, for example, like Paris, marriage would seem to be almost unfashionable, and celibacy to have supplied its place. And this state of things will soon exist in our own country, unless the young can be thoroughly imbued with correct principles on this important subject.

Some shelter themselves under the plea that matrimonial life is so expensive that they cannot maintain it. Once, they say, married life was as cheap as celibacy, for woman was both able and willing to do her part; whereas, now-a-days, most women are either unable or unwilling to do any thing towards supporting a family. Woman, they say, marries now to be maintained; not to help to maintain others.

Others dread the cares and responsibilities which attach to this state of life. They might support one person besides themselves, they say; but as for supporting half-a-dozen or a dozen more, they cannot for one moment think of it. And it cannot be right, they suppose, to be at the head of a family and not take care of it.

Others again dread the confinement. God made me to be free, it is said—as free as the air. I enjoy that freedom; and if I am not very useful in the world, I am sure I do no harm. And now shall I sign away this golden privilege? Shall I confine myself to home all my days? Shall I not, on the contrary, remain free, as God made me?

Others, still, speak of the risk they run. "Marriage is at best but a lottery, in which there are many more blanks than prizes. And when the chance of an even match is so small, and the prospects of an ill-adapted, ill-assorted, unhappy selection, so numerous, why should I dare to adventure? Surely, if we must be miserable, it is better to be miserable alone."

And there are, lastly, those who speak of the evils of perpetuating disease. They have heard that consumption, scrofula, and many more diseases may be transmitted; nay, that the mere bringing together of striking peculiarities, has a tendency that way. But they have heard again, that almost every body is affected by inheritance in some way. And now, say they, what shall we do? You desire us to marry; and yet advise us to avoid the sickly. Is not this to advise, where compliance is impossible?

Now these objections are all of them specious, and a few of them weighty. True, they can be met, and most of them can be shown to be more specious than solid; but to the young, some of them seem formidable. Let us see, then, to what, in reality, they amount, and how great the difficulty is which, to the young, appears so well nigh insurmountable.

Is it true, then, that the wife does not, in modern times, aid in bringing up a family? Does the whole burden devolve on the husband? Or if it is so now, must it continue to be so? If woman is a slave to foolish and hurtful fashions, is there no release? Can she not return at once to those simple habits and customs which prevailed in the last century, and which permitted woman to act her part in matrimonial life, as well as her husband?

You will say, perhaps: But women, now, have not strength for this. Some, yes, many, have not, I grant; but if they can have a little respite from a constant round of drudgery, which is as unreasonable as it is silly, there is hope they may recover their vigor. Besides, there are a few among us who have as yet tolerable constitutions.

And as to care, it is "the stuff that life is made of." More among us are sufferers because they do not have care enough, than because they have too much. Multitudes there are who, if they had somebody to care for, would not prey upon themselves as they now do. I acknowledge there is such a thing as being care-worn; but, upon my word, I find fewer care-worn persons in matrimonial life, than in "single blessedness."

You speak of the risk to be run. This may be greater or less, according to circumstances. If you are governed by wise principles in the selection of a partner for life, the risk is not so great as you may suppose. If reason and judgment predominate over fancy, your success will, after all, be something more certain that of drawing a prize in a lottery!

In forming an estimate of character, for example, you must not expect to come at truth in the concert, or at the ball, or the assembly-room. Here there is, practically, a mask drawn over every thing. To know a person thoroughly, as she truly is, you must see her at home, in the domestic circle. Would you know her temper, you must observe its trials in small matters rather than larger ones. Thousands mistake here, and vainly suppose they understand character, when a borrowed part is acted rather than a real one. It is much easier to govern ourselves on a few great occasions, than in the thousand and one smaller items, of which real practical life is so essentially and so extensively made up.

And, in the next place, you must study adaptation more than young men usually do. It is not by any means necessary that you and your companions should be alike in any thing except general purpose or aim. But it is indispensably necessary that there should be mutual adaptation to each other in a great variety of particulars. Some are of more, (that is, standing by themselves,) others of less importance.

There should be adaptation, physically. One should not be many years older than the other. Not only does much physical, but much social and moral evil, result from inattention to this circumstance. Most men, especially bachelors, are apt to prefer a companion in life, who is considerably younger than themselves; and, strange to say, not a few females prefer those who are older than they.

On the other hand, if one party is tall, experience appears to direct that the other should be rather short; and if one is corpulent, that the other should be comparatively lean. It is still more important that if one be habitually too grave—an error by no means uncommon in this world—the other should be habitually mirthful.

Intellectual adaptation is of little less importance than physical. The one party should make up, so to speak, for deficiencies in the other. I do not mean to say that we should turn Mohammedans, and regard women as made only to *complete* man, or as having no separate, independent existence. And yet it is somewhat as if it were so. Men and women as they now exist, are but mere fragments of human beings, and it requires at least two of them to make up any thing like a decent whole.

Moral and religious adaptation deserves to be considered among the rest. Some have been inclined wholly to omit this subject, in forming an estimate of the character of one whom they would select for life's journey.

This seems to me no part of true wisdom. There must not only be charity in regard to differences of opinion, but the difference must not be *too* great at first setting out. otherwise there will be danger of collision.

And then, finally, those who make the foregoing objections to matrimony, should remember that however plain they may come up before the mind's eye, they must be still more plainly seen by God himself, who ordained matrimony. If, then, in view of all these difficulties, God has said, It is not good for man to be alone, and no repeal has ever been uttered, who shall withstand God? What God has joined together, most surely man may not put asunder.

Besides, the God who ordained matrimony, ordained also the existence of those who are to engage in it. He made them human beings, too, and not angels. And in assigning them their duty, he has nowhere required more of them than they are able to perform. In selecting a companion for life, we are but to do the best we can. And

"Who does the best his circumstance allows,
Does well; acts nobly—angels could no more."

One thought more. I have barely alluded to age. The popular doctrine at present is, that we should marry young. I admit its truth, *but what is young?* In some states of society, twenty-five or thirty would be regarded as such; in others, young would mean twenty or eighteen.

This is a great and an important question. I have barely room to say that I consider twenty-five to twenty-eight, in our own sex, as young enough; and twenty-two to twenty-five, in the other sex. Some, however, are as mature, physically, mentally, and morally, at twenty-five, as others are at twenty-eight. No young man is physically mature much sooner than twenty-five.

Perhaps I owe you an apology, my young friends, for the familiarity with which I treat you and my subject. In a better state of society—one in which fathers did their whole duty—such instruction, from such a source, would not be demanded. Unite, then, your prayers and labors with mine, that such a state of society may one day exist; nay, even that so golden a period mav not be far distant.

LETTER XXXII.

RELIGION AND SKEPTICISM.

Many of you have seen a volume which made its appearance some years since, entitled, "Influence of Religion on Health," by a physician of eminence, containing not a few wholesome truths and important suggestions. And yet, so much has the worthy author confounded false religions with the true, and the abuse of Christianity with its advantages, that you may have risen from the perusal of the work with a stronger tendency towards skepticism, than you had when you sat down. If these are the influences which religion exerts—you may have said to yourselves—then, the less we have to do with it, the better.

Young men, in this country, are naturally

inclined to skepticism. The genius of our institutions favors this tendency; that is, it does so indirectly. Not that there is more skepticism abroad in regard to religion, than in regard to many other things, especially medicine; perhaps not so much—still, there is such a tendency. The freedom of our civil institutions, leads to free thinking. Men cast off many opinions in which they were educated, because they seem to them utterly unfounded; and some, simply *because* they were educated in them. And in passing from one extreme, they are apt to go suddenly to another. In avoiding Scylla, they fall on Charybdis.

It was to such a community, with such tendencies, that the "Influence of Religion on Health" brought an increase of skepticism. It performed a work which, in all probability, was never intended. But the impressions it left on the public mind—so manifestly erroneous—are susceptible of being removed, and ought to be. Religion, pure and undefiled—in other words, Christianity, in its influences on human health and happiness—is very far from being unfavorable. On the contrary, as can be easily shown and clearly demonstrated, godliness is as profitable to this life, as it is for the life to come. And if so, instead of rendering us skeptical, it ought to diminish our skepticism, by affording us one more internal proof, that religion is divine. For, can such a result or tendency, in a world like ours, be a matter of mere chance or hap-hazard? Is there no proof here, of design—nay, more, of benevolent intention?

Let us consider, in the first place, the tendencies of repentance and faith on our present well-being. I take these first, because it is these to which the gospel of our Lord and Saviour first directs our special attention.

In taking the ground that repentance is favorable to health and happiness here, I shall doubtless be met at once by the inquiry: But does not repentance for sin, involve grief and self-loathing, and other feelings of the depressing kind? And can long-continued grief be healthful? The reply to this inquiry is, that the best part of repentance is reformation. It is not necessary, in the nature of things, as God has established them, that we should continue to grieve always; if it were so, the result would most certainly be unfavorable. To live permanently and habitually under the influence of any of the depressing passions, must ever be injurious both to body and soul. So that, after all, to repeat the statement—the best, and indeed the principal part of repentance, is reformation. The essential meaning of the foreign word whence the verb repent is derived, implies, as its leading idea, the act of turning. And to repent of sin, is to turn away from it.

Now, who that has read the catalogue of vices which Paul makes out against the Orientals—and our modern catalogue would not be shorter—before their repentance, will doubt for a moment, whether or not the turning away from these is favorable to health? Can it, by possibility, be otherwise than that to break away from licentiousness, intemperance, and anger, is to promote health and longevity, and thus to add to human happiness?

But if repentance is healthful and salutary, faith is much more so. The faith or confidence of infancy and childhood in parental love, can hardly be over-estimated; and whether it have much or little resemblance to the faith of the child of God—that faith by which Abraham, at the command of his heavenly Father, went out, not knowing whither he went—is as certainly salutary to the body as it is to the soul.

So is that common faith or confidence which men have in the constitution of things—or what we sometimes call nature. The agriculturist who sows or plants his field in full faith, i. e. in full expectancy of a crop, is all the healthier for it. The merchant who, with the same faith, commits his ships to the seas, is a healthier man, other things being equal, than he who is faithless. Such men have a better circulation of the blood—have better lungs, brain, nerves, skin, &c.—than other men, as could be demonstrated.

I know of few things that can conduce more to happiness in this life than faith. It is not merely that it favors bodily health, and thus conduces to longevity, but it tends to bring the mind and soul into that tranquil state for which thousands and thousands sigh in vain. The wicked are as the troubled sea. says the Scripture; and so are the faithless and skeptical. I have been acquainted with many skeptics; and have waded through the wide sea of infidelity myself; and yet I can truly say, I never knew of any peace to the mind under this sort of "wickedness."

Men of this description generally say they are at peace; but facts prove that it is otherwise. I do not refer here to their peace in death, so much as to their peace in life. As men live, so they generally die. It is not true, always, that death-beds are honest places, as many pretend. They are true, generally, to the life. If the life has been an honest life, the death will be equally so. If it has been a peaceful life, its termination will usually be peaceful. If faith has predominated during life, it will prevail in the hour of death.

It is, however, the influence of principles or practices, or opinions on our lives, and not on our deaths, that I have principally to do with. And I say again, that a life of skepticism—even of skepticism in regard to parents, the laws or results of nature, &c.—is a most perturbed and unhappy life. Hume and Voltaire may have been exceptions to the truth of this remark; but then, too, they may not have been. There was a restlessness, at times, about the latter—a sort of desperation—that does not seem much like the peace of the gospel. Admit, however, the most that is claimed for them, in this respect; and yet they stand nearly alone. Besides, these men seem not to have been wholly destitute of that common faith to which I have adverted; and this must have greatly modified their skepticism in regard to God and things heavenly and divine.

But, for one skeptic like Hume and Voltaire, we have thousands and tens of thousands of smaller ones, who, while they have no confidence in any thing in the heavens above, have little more in what pertains to the earth beneath. Little more, did I say? They have not half as much. There is vastly more skepticism in regard to ourselves and those around us, and especially in regard to nature and nature's laws, than there is in regard to a higher, and, as it is usually believed, a more culpable kind.

To illustrate. Voltaire, in early life, could

invest his money in slaves and trust them to the winds and the ocean, and the chances of trade in a capricious market—and he could do it in confidence or faith. I do not say that he had *no* misgivings—that he never for one moment doubted whether the elements might not conspire against him, or at least, whether the winds might not blow unpropitiously; for this were more than could be expected of humanity. But I do mean to say, that with every drawback, and every deduction, his common faith in common things, was in large measure.

I do not know how it may have been in this particular with Hume; but I repeat it, one thing I do know—it is not so with skeptics in general. They are the last men to trust, or be trusted. Doubting and distrusting heaven, they doubt and distrust every thing else. They are timid, fearful, irresolute and capricious. They are fretful, moreover, beyond other men. There is fretfulness enough every where; but it grows in richest profusion in the hot-bed of practical skepticism. Would a young man avoid the world of fretting, let him have faith, even though it were but worldly faith. Let him add, however, to his worldly faith, as a cap to the climax, the faith of the gospel.

I have alluded to fretfulness. By this I do not so much refer to those outbursts which, like Etna and Vesuvius, do large but temporary mischief, as to that internal fretfulness, or continual anxiety and worry with which our earth is filled. Even the professed disciple of Jesus Christ, too often comes much short of the faith and quiet of his great Master. Never such faith as *His*, and never such peace—such freedom from fretfulness, both internal and external.

For, when and where did our great Master manifest fear and trembling, lest the weather should be unfavorable—too hot or too cold; too wet or too dry; or lest winds, seas, or markets, should disappoint his expectations? When and where did he not encourage the same faithfulness in others? Nay, when or where did he neglect to rebuke this same want of faith in those around him? Was it on the sea of Galilee alone that he said to the over-anxious, O ye of little faith? Was he not equally bent on portraying this ever-appearing skepticism, when on the Mount he said to his disciples: Be not anxious (i. e. over-anxious) what ye shall eat, or what ye shall drink?

In this respect, no less than in others, is the young man of Nazareth worthy of being your model. Happy, if you attain, in any good measure, to his divine image. Happy if you have but the tithe of his practical faith. It will be profitable both in this life and that which is to come.

Paul was a most eminent instance of the same virtue. For it cannot have escaped the notice of the most unobserving, that he was full of faith—at least, common faith—before he became a disciple of Him whom at first he opposed. It was his faith in God and nature —and finally in God's own Son—that made him one of the most healthy, vigorous, self-denying, enduring and happy men the world ever saw.

No wonder the Bible-writers lay so much stress on faith. No wonder the Apostle Paul recounts with so much pleasure the doings and sufferings of those who were stoned, torn asunder, tempted, slain with the sword—who wandered about in sheep-skins and goat-skins, being destitute, afflicted, tormented, scourged, shipwrecked, killed all the day long, &c.—of whom, as he says, the world was not worthy. No wonder he was himself a host in the cause of man and of God. So would every young man be, with Paul's repentance and faith, especially the latter. And well might the Apostle affirm to Timothy, that godliness hath promise of the life that now is, no less than of that which is to come.

LETTER XXXIII.

THE CHRISTIAN RELIGION.

It is not possible to mistake, when we say that our young men are inclined to skepticism. The genius of our institutions, and the general tendencies of things, favor such a result. Nor is it the part of wisdom to come down upon the young, in a species of vengeance, because they entertain doubts on religious subjects. It were wiser to take a different course. Let us rather, in the language of holy writ, "reason together."

Nothing is more common than the remark that belief is safe, because if the truths believed in should prove to be but the "baseless fabric of a vision"—a mere delusion—the delusion is a pleasant one; and we shall, at least, be as well off in the great future as the opposer of Christianity; whereas, if religion should be true, we shall of course be safe. Now, such remarks as these, however common, appear to me not only idle, but despicable. One who was far from being very orthodox in his sentiments has said, "An honest man's the noblest work of God"—what, then, of a dishonest man? And what but dishonesty—downright hypocrisy—is it to pretend to believe what we do not believe, under the idea that it is safe? Safe to be dishonest—hypocritical? Perish such a sentiment! Let it revert to the bottomless pit, whence it came!

If our religion—the Christian religion—be true, it ought to be sustained by proper evidence. If otherwise, if it cannot be thus sustained, then I, for one, say to every young man in the world, Reject it. God never meant you should receive that which you honestly think unworthy of your reception. You may not, indeed, have examined the evidence he has placed in your way; and herein may be culpable. But I say again, it would be the strange administration of a still stranger sovereign, who should so arrange things as to require his subjects to believe against their honest convictions, after a perfect and candid investigation.

If it can be shown, to the entire satisfaction of my readers, that the doctrines, duties and graces of Christianity, in their practical application to daily life, as well as its institutions (when not perverted), are as beneficial to the body as to the soul—favorable, in short, to man's every interest, here and hereafter, is there not, even in this, an indication of its divine origin?

We have seen, in former articles, that the repentance and faith to which the Gospel calls us, are not unfavorable to human health and longevity—and that the latter is even highly favorable. But the Gospel requires us to add to our faith a long list of other qualities or virtues—such as love, hope, peace, joy, temperance, purity, doing good, &c. It sanctions marriage, the church, the Sabbath, religious training, and indeed whatever may be said to be pure, lovely and of good report.

Now, if it could happen by any remarkable coincidence, that though Christianity was a fable or humbug, yet some one or two of these—as faith and repentance—were favorable to health and longevity, it could hardly happen that the whole list which I have enumerated would be. Such an agreement would be more than chance or hap-hazard. It would be the harmony of truth; and would be a strong argument, a very strong one, in favor of our religion. Indeed it seems to me an argument which few, if any, would attempt to gainsay or resist.

And yet it *can* be shown, most clearly, that all the virtues above, as enjoined or sanctioned by Christianity, together with its doctrines and institutions, are as favorable to the happiness of mankind, even in this life, as if this state of probation were all; as if our motto should everywhere be, "Let us eat and drink," let us enjoy the present moment, "for to-morrow we die." It is not repentance and faith alone, but the whole list of elevating affections and passions. It is every thing, in short, which tends to make us representatives of our Lord and Saviour Jesus Christ.

I shall be met here, I know, with the

common objection—How happens it, then, if the graces, virtues and institutions of Christianity *are* favorable to health, that so many of those who profess to be influenced by it, especially its ministers, are gloomy, sickly, or short-lived?

But this objection assumes two things as true which are manifest errors. First: it confounds the *profession* of piety with the *practice* of it, whereas it is too well known that they do not always go together. Second: It takes for granted that there is an efficacy in piety to restore immediate health and cheerfulness, which none of its most zealous advocates would claim. Besides, it assumes, as proved, what some may well be supposed to deny, and what has certainly never yet *been* proved, that the *piety* of gospel ministers *renders them sickly.*

For nothing is plainer, with regard to Christian ministers, than that they are badly educated. The world is, indeed, full of miseducation—but on no class do its evils fall so unsparingly as on ministers. They are selected while mere boys, as a very general fact, from the ranks of the nervous, the scrofulous, the consumptive or the dyspeptic. And then their treatment through their whole course, is just such as it should be if those who direct their destiny were fully determined to set all physical law at defiance. And yet, in spite of all this, we have a few healthy ministers; and more than a few who have health enough to render them exceedingly useful in their profession. Perhaps, as a whole, they are nearly as healthy as most other classes of men, in spite of all the unfavorable tendencies by which they are surrounded.

And as to common Christians, it should not be forgotten that, for the most part, the voice of mercy is not heard by them till their health, though it may have been tolerable by inheritance, is ruined, or nearly so, by the various forms of physical and moral transgression to which they have been more or less subjected. It is not for Christianity, in these latter days at least, to perform miracles. It does not take possession of the individual in a pure or healthy state, but takes him as he is, deformed and diseased by sin, and strives to make him better. But the changes it works are not, in every instance, very rapid. The improvement it proffers is for the *race*, rather than for the *individual*. If in the present generation, but two per cent. be gained, it is very much. The next generation, with the same efforts, means and principles, can gain five per cent.; the next ten, and so on. All-powerful as piety is, and even all healthy as it is, it can hardly elevate those angles of the mouth which have been depressed for a score or two of years by ungovernable passions or by continued fretfulness. Nor can it smooth the brow that, by the same causes, has been knit for years in wrinkles and frowns. Nor can it change in a moment or a month that temperament, which, once happily balanced between the sanguine and nervous, has become deeply tinged, even to bilious disease, by a predominance of the angry passions.

While, therefore, I claim for religion—the Christian religion I mean, of course—a power almost unlimited in its tendencies to health, I do not, I again say, claim for it any thing miraculous. All I maintain and hold myself competent to prove is, that its whole tendency, and the tendency of all its parts is to human health, and every form of temporal happiness. It is not given us merely to *die* by, it is equally useful to *live* by. If it were not so, it would need one more proof than we now possess of its superiority over Mohammedanism, or even Paganism. But if it be thus—if it be healthy and life-giving—if its every virtue and every precept are as favorable to the well-being of the body as to that of the soul, then we have an argument for its divinity not to be found elsewhere, and one which, as I have already said, is unanswerable.

I am the more particular in stating the argument as above, because it will be new to some, and also because the facts have not been in every instance correctly presented. The author of "The Influence of Religion on Health," whom I quoted in a former letter, though a professed believer in Christianity, so confounded Christianity pure and undefiled, with its abuses, and even other forms of religion with the true, as to leave the unhappy, and perhaps unintended impression, that the latter itself was not healthful, but the contrary. And I most fully believe that the effect of this very learned and ingenious work, was to produce a very general belief in the minds of a multitude of the young, that the whole matter was one of very doubtful utility, so far, at least, as this world's happiness is concerned; that if religion is useful to die by, it is of little consequence—rather none at all—to live by. In other words, its tendency was, as I conceive, to infidelity.

LETTER XXXIV.

DEATH AND FUTURITY.

There has been almost as much speculation on the subject of death as on that of life. Philosophy, physiology, mesmerism and morality, have all failed to tell us what either is. The only satisfactory information we seem to have concerning them, is derived from the Scriptures.

One thing we do know, however, that both *are*—that we *live*, and that we *die*. Whether originally designed to live a hundred, a thousand, or ten thousand years—or whether to die at all—is not the question. All that are now on the stage of human existence—all that have been born—must sooner or later die. It is a warfare from which there is no discharge.

Some tell us that the time, manner, place,

&c., of our death, are of no consequence; that as we live, so we shall die. That if we live well we shall die well; but that if we live ill, we must die ill. At least this is, as they say, the general rule.

Others make every thing of the circumstances connected with death. They measure a person's spiritual worth almost wholly by the manner of his exit. If he dies in agitation, or fear, they set him down as a bad man; but if he dies joyfully—in expectation of heaven—then there is hope in his death.

Just views on this subject would probably lead us midway between these two extremes. It is true on the one hand, that as we live, so are we apt to die; but it is equally true, that a happy death-bed is desirable. Who does not love to see the sun set pleasantly? Who does not love to be happy and to see others happy in all the circumstances and events of existence—and is not death *one* of them?

I counsel you, my dear friends, to entertain just views of death and dying. Not that it may cast a gloom over your feelings; but for the very reason that it may *not.* It is not they who never think of death—but always shrink from it—during life, that die with the most composure; but those as a general rule who make it a subject of frequent reflection.

Death is not, of course, the blotting out of any of our powers. It is, at most, a change. Job calls it a change of countenance. Is it much more? We are not sure—quite sure—that even the body *ceases to be.* Most look for a resurrection—the reunion of soul and body—and not a few suppose they are to have, in the resurrection, not merely *a* body, but *the* body;—the very same body which they lay down in the grave.

I shall not of course enter upon any discussion of this great subject, though it might be interesting. All I contend for now, is, that death is only a change; and so far as we can see, a slight one. It is merely the putting on of immortality. It is, as it were, the fabled Styx which we must cross. It is the gate that leads to the celestial city—at least if ever we arrive there. It opens to us the portals of the eternal world, whether we are to be happy there, or miserable.

I have said that death is a change—but of what? Is it a change of character, or even accompanied or immediately followed by any such change? This is a belief into which some young men fall. But beware of such a fallacy. As the tree falls, so it lies; whether towards the north or towards the south, where it falls, there it shall be.

Many solace themselves, now-a-days, with the idea that a great and beneficial change passes upon all men, as soon as they "pass the bounds of time and space." But is it necessary for me to say that such a notion accords as ill with reason, as with Revelation? Need I repeat what I have said elsewhere, that no miracle will be wrought at death, or subsequently, to make you fit for a state of happiness for which you have not with God's help already prepared yourselves?

Is death a change of place? This we cannot certainly know. The idea of passing the bounds of time and space, in the last paragraph, is a poet's idea, and not a Christian's.

We know not whether heaven and hell are all around us, so to speak,—a world within a world—as chariots and horses were round about the man in the days of Elijah and Elisha, though he saw them not till his eyes were opened; and we know not, on the other hand, but there are literally mansions for the blessed as well as dungeons or pits for the miserable. Our modern theology that would teach us heaven and hell are holy and unholy characters—states, and not places—may be little more true than that of a thousand years ago, which taught of streets literally paved with gold on one hand, and a literal lake of fire on the other. Future ages may learn, perchance, not to be wise on this subject, above what is written.

Let us, then, return to our first position. "Thou changest his countenance, and sendest him away," said the ancient; and this is nearly all which is known of change at death to the moderns. The *mode* of our existence—the externals of it—are changed; let us stop at this point, and study humility before we proceed further.

One thing we do know, however, that we are made susceptible of everlasting and inconceivable progress, both intellectually and morally—it may be physically. And what we are made capable of, we have sufficient motive to become. We know not yet what we shall be, said the beloved John to his spiritual brethren. And may I not, in my own humble sphere and way, say the same thing to you?

You are ambitious;—I had almost said, you ought to be. Certainly you were made to soar aloft in pursuit of something. Your noble nature was never given that you might creep like the serpent and lick the dust. "Man *must* soar," said the poet Young. And is it not so? Is he worthy the name of man who is so degraded as not to desire to rise, and rise, and rise, where Gabriel and Raphael, in their upward flight, are yet strangers? But I have said enough of this in other letters.

This is a world of preparation; a world where we are to learn the first rudiments of the art of flying amid the hosts of heaven, and, as connected by faith with the Author of the Christian scheme, of rising higher than any other created beings. Here we are first to spread those pinions, which after death are to become free and full of immortality.

Now every act of your lives, however small, bears in this view upon your eternal progress in knowledge and happiness. It is, however, one thing to know, and quite another to love and obey, and enjoy the reward of obedience. It is one thing to fly upward, with increasing speed through everlasting ages, a missionary of good to all; and another to fly into thicker and yet thicker darkness and ignominy, through ages interminable, dragging downward at the same time as many others as you can. Satan knows enough—but alas! Satan is Satan still, despite of knowledge. He has been so for thousands of past years, he will doubtless be so for thousands of ages to come.

Will you not, then, think much concerning the future? I do not ask you to think much of death, though I dare not counsel you to overlook it. But I ask you—I urge you—mainly to think of life. Oh, this Life! I sometimes wonder what death is, and heave a sigh on account of it. For once, however, that I think of death, and sigh, I think a hundred times of life. Oh, the responsibility of living—and of living on eternally—and of eternally living for others!

Have you thought much on this subject? You have thought no doubt of California. You have even thought of going thither. But why? Is it not because you seek happiness? And yet it is a long way to California—its golden sands are all to you in the future—to gain them will cost you weeks and months of preparation, and perhaps of privation. You know this; you knew it when you first thought of California, and half resolved to go there. Did preparation or privation much daunt you? Or was it the uncertainty of all things?

But suppose this uncertainty were all removed. Suppose that by one year, or even two or three of preparation, you could be sure of success. Suppose you could know that after a probation of three years—a mere subsistence and many trials—you could dig from the valley of the Sacramento and bring to your own home

$100,000. Would the long preparation at all daunt you?

Let me, then, direct you to a land as much more desirable than California, as a means of making you happy, as can well be conceived. Think of a land 1500 miles square, so abounding in gold that its streets are paved with it! A land, too, of which, with all its gold, you may have full possession after a few short years of preparation, and without any real privation at all.

Is not such a land desirable? I have spoken as if you might become its sole possessor. But I mean not quite so much. A different law obtains in that bright abode, from what obtains just now in California. In the latter place the great strife at present is to be richer than the rest; and every increase of one's own wealth above that of others, though it sets them at a greater distance from him, seems to add to his happiness. That is to say he is neither happy nor rich in proportion as he sees others rise, and aids them in the work of progress, but exactly the reverse.

Whereas in the new city of which I have

spoken, every one is richer and happier in proportion as others are made rich. Instead, moreover, of but one king, there all are kings and priests, and that for ever and ever. Instead of a contest who shall rule and reign, whether gold or strength, the great question is who shall serve most, and most effectually.

Is not this golden city—this New Jerusalem—worthy of your highest aspirations and highest efforts? Will you not, then, take right views of Death and Futurity? And knowing in what consists your highest interest and the will of God, and that these are in everlasting harmony, will you not be wise—wise for time and wise for eternity?

www.ingramcontent.com/pod-product-compliance
Lightning Source LLC
LaVergne TN
LVHW020233110826
845151LV00003B/906

9781425530433